NOT
IN THE
CLUB

NOT
IN THE
CLUB

An Executive Woman's Journey Through the
Biased World of Business

JANET PUCINO

East Baton Rouge Parish Library
Baton Rouge, Louisiana

Not In The Club
An Executive Woman's Journey Through the Biased World of Business
by Janet Pucino

Deep Canyon Media LLC
433 N. Camden, Suite 600, Beverly Hills, CA 90210
Phone: 424-666-9401

www.DeepCanyonMedia.com
Info@DeepCanyonMedia.com

Copyright © 2012 by Janet Pucino
All rights reserved. No part of this publication may be reproduced, distributed, or transmitted in any form or by any means, or stored in a database or retrieval system, without the prior written permission of the publisher except in the case of brief quotations embodied in critical articles and reviews.

ISBN: 978-0-9859027-1-1 (Hardbound)
ISBN: 978-0-9859027-0-4 (Softbound)

Library of Congress Control Number: 2012946226

First Edition, Printed in the United States of America
0987654321

Book Design by www.KarrieRoss.com
Author and cover photograph by Starla Fortunato
Chapter photographs provided by iStockphoto.com

TABLE OF CONTENTS

ABOUT THE AUTHOR

AS A HIGHLY EXPERIENCED INFORMATION Technology (IT) executive, Janet Pucino has designed and implemented leading technologies across a broad range of industries, including media and entertainment, financial services, health insurance, and technology. Throughout her executive career she ran every facet of IT, including strategic planning, application development and service delivery, risk management, enterprise architecture, quality assurance, project management, program and change management, strategic labor sourcing and outsourcing, network design, and end user computing support.

Janet held many senior level positions throughout her career. She was a Corporate VP and the highest-ranking female executive in the IT Division of a globally recognized media and entertainment conglomerate. While there, she became an executive sponsor for a women's affinity group that focused on career development for women across the company, an experience that formalized her interest in mentorship and professional development for women.

She was the Chief Technology Officer at a prestigious design college, where she was responsible for developing and implementing a strategic technology plan for film, digital media, graphic and product design, and for providing IT services in support of all design programs. Janet was the President and Founder of a management consulting company, where she successfully delivered quality IT solutions to notable corporate clients around the world. She managed quality and continuous improvement for a first-generation wireless data company, and launched new networks, applications and technologies for financial services and insurance firms in Fortune 1000 companies. Throughout her career, she drew on her passion for IT while mentoring and developing her staff along the way.

Janet received her MBA from the University of Chicago Booth School of Business and received her undergraduate degree from Northern Illinois University. She serves on the Chicago Booth Advisory Council and is a featured speaker at industry and academic conferences.

She is currently the CEO and Founder of Deep Canyon Media LLC, a content development, publishing, and consulting company in southern California.

--

It's Not You

WOMEN REPRESENT OVER 50% OF THE labor pool in the U.S. While a number have risen to top levels in corporate U.S.-based organizations (e.g., Pepsico, Xerox, Kraft Foods, Campbell Soup Company), statistically they are exceptions at the executive levels and in boardrooms.[1] Even when women reach the uppermost echelons in business, they seldom become a member of "The Club" to which their male counterparts belong; The Club is the group that values its members' contributions and surrounds them with a social network of power that leads them to opportunities and financial success.

This book looks at the impact of The Club's culture from a woman's perspective. At the core, this is a personal reflection of my 30-year journey in information technology (IT) management across various industries, with the goal of raising awareness regarding the distinct experiences of women in the workplace as they advance toward executive positions. I hope to call attention to the behaviors and organizational cultures that continue to hinder women's progress toward leadership positions, and to illustrate the need for inclusion and parity in our society and organizations whether corporate, governmental, or non-profit in structure. Corporate and societal changes need to occur now. Although I spent most of my management career in IT in large organizations, my experiences and conclusions about those experiences are applicable to every discipline and every type of organization — large and small.

— □ —

... women are treated differently from men for reasons that extend beyond their biological differences.

— □ —

I hope to inspire both women and men by providing a personal view of the road I traveled to the executive suite that others can follow and that will bring their talent, creativity, productivity, and most of all personal satisfaction to the forefront of their personal lives as well as careers. Over the course of my management career, I have been enlightened by many female and male colleagues as well as friends along the way. I have referenced their stories as a way to further define The Club's attributes and affects. Undoubtedly, I've been a salmon swimming upstream for three decades. However, my experiences in the workplace were not as unique as I thought them to be, as my colleague's parallel experiences illustrate, and as the U.S. labor and gender research now shows.

Biologically women are different from men. No surprises there. But women are treated differently from men in the work place for reasons that extend beyond their biological differences. We can't escape our social context and situations; nor should we be expected to change ourselves to conform to a corporate or hierarchical organizational paradigm in order to be accepted in a men's club culture. Instead, I wish to use my experiences and those of my colleagues to encourage women to look beyond themselves when confronted by puzzling behaviors from their male counterparts—which I can predict with a high level of certainty will occur throughout a woman's career. I also hope that this book helps women in several ways – preparing them for the professional challenges they may encounter, guiding them through barriers and challenging behaviors, and encouraging them to feel confident about asking for the critical elements of success, namely the financial and structural elements that are vital to their career advancement and personal lives. This applies equally to women who are just starting their career journeys and those who are experienced professionals. Women have to make trade-offs during their careers to accommodate life's larger goals, just as men do. However, women are often economically and hierarchically penalized because of outdated views and calculations regarding their contributions to a company.

I wanted to approach the writing of this book as an experienced manager and executive, rather than a researcher.

Nevertheless, references to key research on gender biases, women's experiences, and human behaviors are provided throughout the book. Remarkable work already exists by notable academic researchers and professors such as Rosabeth Moss Kanter, Kristen Schilt, Christopher Hsee, and Mary Lou Schmidt, to name just a few. I was quite surprised to see how much data on gender experiences and inequality, across multiple industries, was analyzed and published during my management career, particularly since these data had virtually no impact on corporate structures, labor laws, governmental policies or business programs in the top business schools. The research findings strikingly mirror many of my personal experiences as a management practitioner as well as those of my female colleagues. The lack of attention to women's nascent presence in leadership roles is conspicuous by its absence in all organizations — academia, political organizations, corporate America — and its lack of coverage in the media.

— □ —

...men control the pace at which women will be allowed into leadership positions

— □ —

It's as if millions of trees have fallen in the forest and nobody heard them. I want to assure women *and men* who are not in The Club that "it's not you!" Although I don't speak for every woman executive, I can offer an examination of real work experiences that are relatable and thought-provoking to a broad audience.

I use the term 'heuristics' throughout the book because it is often used by behavioral scientists to describe the process of accumulating knowledge or arriving at a conclusion based on one's own personal experience. Heuristics is a process humans regularly engage in to make a decision, or to validate and calibrate one's views, which could result in bias if one's individual experiences are limited. To avoid the human tendency to use heuristics as intuitive judgment by relying on my experiences in the workplace to extrapolate common experiences among executive women, I have also included feedback from male executives who volunteered their experiences working with and for women in the book. This male perspective provides valuable insight into the core differences between men and women and how they are perceived in the workplace. While writing this book with a female audience in mind, I unexpectedly discovered that many of the men I interviewed related to the stories about Club behavior from either having personally experienced similar situations at some point in their career, or in knowing other men who exhibited Club behaviors. Although my book comes from a female voice and speaks to women in varying stages of their careers, it also attempts to raise awareness in men about how certain beliefs and behaviors stifle opportunities for women and negatively impact the institutions they may be leading. Given that men maintain critical mass in leadership positions, they control the evolution of their organizational cultures and the pace at which women will be allowed into leadership positions.

My experiences were formulative for me, and each position I held in my career led to the next. Each position, role, and challenge developed strength and management acumen, and I wouldn't change any of the choices I made. I now have great appreciation for the need for military recruits to go through boot camp! Women achieving leadership roles reminds me of boot camp in that we've grown "by doing it the hard way." When you're Not In The Club, where do you turn when there is a noticeable lack of mentors, low representation of women in leadership roles, few management books that target a woman's experience as she ascends into senior leadership positions, and lack of diversity-focused education in most graduate business programs? Once I stepped into an executive-level position, I had a much deeper appreciation for what I, and other women executives, had accomplished and what guidance I could offer to aspiring executives.

Many of the women and students I've mentored over the years have asked me to describe the top actions, choices and solutions that worked for me. So as not to oversimplify a complex set of views across multiple disciplines in management, labor economics, behavioral science, sociology and psychology, I have steered away from reducing my experiences and my colleagues' experiences to a formula, or a program for success, and instead I've approached them as a Rubik's cube, with many facets.

I'd like to see an end to the "Top Ten 'Must Do'" lists published in business journals and magazines that point out all of the supposed defects that women need to fix within themselves to achieve success. I can say confidently that women have done more than enough to prove they are educated, able, and worthy of leadership positions. As of 2010, women received 61% of MBAs and were on par with men in obtaining their doctorate degrees.[2] Women have already figured out how to manage their careers and their families, although they are still being economically penalized for their time spent raising children. With insights from several scholars and professors at the University of Chicago and UCLA, I am able to look back with a pedantic lens at my experiences and those of my peers, and

I can render a more informed prescription for the changes that need to take place in our boardrooms and organizational structures—and within our culture—rather than merely instructing women to simply help themselves.

A book about the roadblocks women still face in moving up to senior leadership roles and board positions seems to strike a loud and occasionally visceral chord with the individuals with whom I've discussed the relevant issues (such as the Lethal Barriers [Chapter 3], developing the Critical Elements of Success [Chapter 6], and the Prescriptions Women Need Now [Chapter 8]). The reactions ranged from a cringe-worthy "oh no, not one of those books" comment, to a recommendation to tone down the message so I wouldn't "take any heat," and more. Some of the academics I interviewed made it clear upfront in our discussion that they "didn't do gender studies." One male Chief Executive Officer (CEO) I interviewed just didn't believe the data showing that in 2010, women comprised about 3% of CEO positions in Fortune 500 companies. However, many of the women and men I engaged had stories to tell about Club-based organizations, and they freely shared their personal experiences with me. One veteran male executive at an aerospace firm said his company made a concerted effort in the early 2000s to develop a more diverse workforce and raise awareness of the lack of women engineers in their firm. He said that before then, "no one really thought about it." It is surprising or even astounding on some levels that a company would begin addressing this issue only within the last ten years. It seems that both men and women have adapted to, and perhaps even accepted, women's minority presence in many industries without challenging the status quo of The Club.

However, what I have learned through hard work, rigor, and the male perspective is that wanting to be in The Club leads to a diminishing return of reward and personal satisfaction. Other alternatives and actions must be considered to address the largely untapped intellectual capital of women in the labor pool, which impacts their ability to contribute to the GDP and economic growth in the U.S. I offer insights into the many ways that situational contexts (how men and women are socially presented and perceived) and gender biases affect decision-making in the workplace, and I provide organizational prescriptions to prevent patterns of behavior that foster negative aspects of Club behavior. I believe that anyone, regardless of gender or uniqueness, will recognize their context and status with The Club at their workplace. I hope that my experiences will help the readers of this book forge a successful career, as they have for me and many of my colleagues.

CHAPTER 1:

The Club —
In Corporate Organizations
and Everywhere Else

A LOOK BACK OVER MY 30 YEARS IN management affords me an excellent opportunity to recognize both the cultures and behaviors that made a significant contribution to my success and well-being, as well as the environmental and behavioral attributes that feed and nurture The Club. What exactly is a Club-based organization, and what does it have to do with your career? It's not a simple undertaking to define the aspects of business environments, circumstances, and people that create The Club culture. I will start by saying there are discernible patterns and behaviors that create a specialness or uniqueness among a club's members regardless of the club's purpose. Clubs by their very nature entice people to cross some threshold to become a member, and clubs in the generic sense aren't inherently bad in hierarchical organizations. It's when a 'club' crosses the threshold and becomes 'The Club' that women begin to experience startling behaviors and barriers in their careers.

Conformance

Groups of people in a company can and do hold common beliefs without adhering to the confines of a Club per se. For example, there are many social, philanthropic and special interest groups hosted by corporations that don't produce Club behavior, and yet they instill a level of conformance and common behaviors across an organization. One of my first experiences in conforming to a common belief and "crossing the threshold" came during the late '80s. Several corporations I worked for required every employee to attend a film depicting all of the ways the charity United Way helps those in need. Attendance was checked to insure that everyone got the message. If you didn't attend the first session, you were hounded for weeks until you attended one of the make-up sessions. The marketers behind United Way were quite clever in using the film to arouse charitable giving in a public forum, particularly one sponsored by your employer. The idea was to collect as many financial commitments to the charity before the employees left the room — commitments which the company then deducted from the employees' paychecks.

United Way successfully leveraged companies' involvement in those campaigns, and although every employee was expected to conform to this standard, the campaigns were based on *inclusion* rather exclusion, and had a positive effect on the organization and individuals. Everyone ultimately felt good (and at times emotional) about giving to a worthy cause, and they wanted their managers to recognize that they were "in" on the giving process. United Way continues to partner with Fortune 100 and 500 companies, because their mission to educate and heal those in need appeals to many corporations that want to foster a philanthropic community within their own organizations.

Negative Aspects of a Club

The negative effects of Club behavior and thinking, which are explored in more detail throughout this book, are quite harmful to individuals and organizations. Negative Club behaviors can easily emerge from management teams who develop "group-think" tendencies, those deep-seated biases or convictions that often prevent new ideas and solutions from being considered and which ultimately lead to less than optimal outcomes. The behaviors and convictions of the senior management team at Enron started in this fashion. Many of the male executives willingly accepted the explanations for Enron's sources of revenue and ignored the signs of financial distress while the business model failed. Sherron Watkins, who was outside The Club, was the noted female whistleblower who revealed the misstatements in the financial reports — because no one closely aligned with then-CEO Jeffrey Skilling's inner circle would have broken with Club protocol and called out the nefarious behavior. Although the memo Sherron Watkins wrote to her senior management team outlining accounting improprieties was not initially acknowledged by them, her message was ultimately heard during the ensuing criminal trials.

For the women and men who are operating on the outer perimeter of the Club as Ms. Watkins was, it's important to recognize when one's ideas and output are being silenced or overlooked, and to decide whether making changes within ourselves, such as acquiring a new skill, developing better rapport, or adjusting our communication styles can have an impact on how our contributions are perceived by The Club. In Ms. Watkins' case, there was nothing more she could have done to influence Jeffrey Skilling's Club.

— □ —

You won't find The Club on an organization chart.

— □ —

A male executive I interviewed for this book spent two years at a large business unit in a Fortune 500 company, and he described his negative experience as a Club outsider in a unique way. His perception of the Club was that it had a "gang-up mentality" that blocked all ideas that were different from the Club's and that the Club exhibited "tribal power" because it was a faction within his company's organizational hierarchy that had its own political agenda. He observed the "tribe" using its power to influence ideas and outcomes, while diluting the Club leader's and Club members' accountability for results. Consequently, it was difficult for him to determine who to take direction from, and who was really "in charge."

Simply put, The Club is comprised of a group of people in an organization who may or may not have direct power over other individuals, and yet the group shepherds its members to new growth opportunities and career advancement. You won't find The Club on an organization chart. It exists in the group of individuals who freely share information and value each others' contributions no matter how small those contributions may be. The members of The Club never fail, in the sense that they don't recognize failure as such. Rather, those who are "in" are exempt from failure and in some cases even continue to be rewarded for poor performance. External forces or those who are outside The Club carry the burden of mistakes. Who wouldn't want to be in a club that treats each of its members that way?

I will quickly dispel any desire you may have to break into that Club. Unless you have a mentor from The Club bringing you along, or you have attributes that are very similar to those of The Club members, it's not likely that you'll become a member. I'll discuss the impact of a mentor later, but it's important to note early on that the attributes of Club members are not limited to men. A non-diverse group of women who block participation and new ideas can also have detrimental effects on an organization. For example, during my tenure as a CTO (chief technology officer), I worked for an organization where the President filled many leadership roles with mostly female employees from his previous organization. He had developed long-term, Club relationships with these employees, having traveled extensively with them at his previous post. He relied on those relationships in his new position, regardless of the areas of expertise his Club members brought to the table.

This turned out to be an organizational model which simply could not sustain the fundamental mission of the institution. This Club thrived on the constant inflow of ideas from each member, which was a big plus for creative thinking and a tremendous learning opportunity for me, but the organization was in need of functional skills alignment, prioritization and management rigor to achieve the aggressive business expansion plan the President had to deliver to his constituents and to the Board of Directors. Unfortunately, the expansion never materialized. Although there were extenuating factors, without becoming a sharply skilled and diverse functional team, the closely knit Club could not achieve the institution's vision.

Positive Aspects of a Club

Opportunities

All Clubs require conformance to a set of rules, or in the case of a corporate club, a code of conduct. The conduct varies greatly, from engaging in pastimes such as golf to attending social events on Friday afternoons, for example, 'greasy cheeseburger' lunches with a pitcher of beer. The more time The Club members spend together, the easier it is for an individual to calibrate his or her behavior with that of the other club members.

At a financial and insurance services company I worked for in the mid-1980s, I really did attend 'greasy cheeseburger' lunches that included the senior levels of management. We didn't meet every single Friday, but there were plenty of opportunities to join this lunch group. One of the more senior managers would just walk around the halls and ask managers if they wanted to attend. These get-togethers were known as 'greasy cheeseburger' lunches because they were always held at a small dive nearby where the atmosphere was perfect for comfortable conversation. The burgers were great too. Since this was the first company to promote me into a line management job, I readily attended.

Because this particular Club was much more inclusive than exclusive, the effects were remarkably positive for me. For starters, my productivity increased. I willingly worked longer hours and even looked forward to Saturday work on occasion. Why? Because I felt comfortable in my surroundings and because everyone at the lunch table, regardless of rank, respected each other and most importantly, remained approachable at the conclusion of lunch. Because I had become a known entity in The Club, I was also given many opportunities that stretched my management skills and challenged me technically. As a result, a new remote agency network was born from the seed of an idea discussed over many lunches, to reduce costs while using state-of-the-art network services.

Access

The premise of a team-based organization was embodied in those lunches. I must underscore that organizational behavior is comprised of individuals' behavior, nurtured by a few top executives. [The many ways that senior management sets the tone in an organization are explored in Chapter 4.] Fortunately for me, the CEO at the company was a mentor to my boss (who, by the way, was a woman), and they both set the example of team work *across the company*. Although there was some resistance from a few of the top managers to accept the newest managers in their workplace sphere, the tone from the top was clear. Most of the senior management team showed up just so they could be at that lunch table with the CEO and his team.

However, within this same company there were two formal social organizations, officially titled the "Women's Club" and the "Men's Club." Really. As it turned out, many women preferred the social outings offered by the Men's Club over those designed to appeal to women. One of the events the Men's Club hosted was a hot dog and beer fest with a Bears defensive lineman who mingled and signed autographs during dinner. Several of us asked to attend that event, and the CEO endorsed it. From that point forward, all Men's Club events were open to women. What changed at the moment organizationally was that women gained greater exposure to decision-makers, influencers and the A-team than they'd had in the past, and they could begin forming relationships that were necessary for success in the company.

Talent and Drive Aren't Enough

The need to have talent and drive is a given, but The Club will determine whether your ideas will be heard and implemented. Geoff Colvin, author of "Talent Is Overrated: What Really Separates World-Class Performers from Everyone Else?" suggests that great performers are influenced and mentored at an early age, and that they understand the value of practicing meaningfully throughout their lives. They don't mindlessly hit buckets of golf balls or practice their instrument for hours every day; they are mindful of every action and every result. They also rely on feedback and recalibrate themselves after failure.[3] In a typical corporate or hierarchical Club environment, however, most women won't have access to mentors, will seldom receive feedback, and won't have the opportunity to fail and recalibrate the way a Club member would.

I realize now that the financial and insurance services company where I worked was not the typical business culture, but my experiences there did guide me as I formulated my "must-haves" to achieve my professional goals, particularly as a woman in management.

I've mentioned key patterns and behaviors associated with The Club, and I want to provide insight into what those patterns look like, sound like, and *feel* like, to help you assess whether you are fully engaging your brain power and skills in your current environment, and whether there are external factors that are impeding your performance. If your gut is telling you something is askew, chances are it is. If you feel like Sisyphus pushing the same boulder up a hill each day, with no carts, horses, pulleys, etc. behind you, it's time to re-examine the culture and your relationship to it. Work doesn't need to be that difficult and unproductive.

— □ —

…most women won't have access to mentors.

— □ —

My most enlightened moment about working hard came during a Technolink Association Conference in 2008.[4] During the conference, one of the flight system engineering managers for the Mars Science Laboratory at Jet Propulsion Labs spoke about the history of the MARS Rover exploration project and the complexities associated with coordinating multiple project teams and scientists working on specific aspects of the launch. She concluded by showing a slide of all the team members cheering when the Rover made its successful touch down on Mars. Afterward I asked her what critical management tool or software application was used to manage the complexity and keep track of the tasks and testing. Given my IT background, I assumed they were relying on a highly sophisticated project management software product.

She said quite simply that the most important factor was the collective teams' focus on finding solutions to problems and their willingness to share and vet all ideas. The teams conversed regularly, and every team knew the status of the other teams' deliverables. If a rocket science project can be a successful and rewarding experience for a diverse team of scientists, so should a woman's career in every corporate organization on the planet.

Assessing Performance

As women ascend the ranks of management and take on more demanding leadership roles, the feedback mechanisms and performance assessments begin to falter. By the time you are a senior-level manager, department chair, or firm partner, feedback from peers and your boss can be indirect or nascent. Having a gauge to assess your experiences and surroundings will help determine whether the challenges you face are a result of your own behavior, or are cultural in nature, or a mixture of both.

Part of the problem with assessing performance objectively stems from the reward systems within a company. Although performance-based pay is often favored by shareholders and employers, such a reward system is difficult to implement for executives who do not touch the manufacturing lines or directly sell products or services, or create technologies. Measuring the results that senior executives are responsible for is tricky and often subjective. According to Dr. David Lewin, Professor at the UCLA Anderson School of Management, research in the area of CEO compensation consistently finds positive, statistically significant relationships between the size of organizations and the CEOs' total compensation and between company verticality (typically, the number of management levels they oversaw) and CEO compensation—rather than on true objective criteria.[5]

– □ –

...the negative impact of the traditional executive pay models on women executives is significant.

– □ –

Whether intentional or not, the negative impact of the traditional executive pay models on women executives is significant as they are not given the same opportunities to oversee large organizations, even though as a group they are more educated than their male peers and represent 50% of the U.S. workforce.[6] In reviewing the census data from 2011, I was struck by how much women have gained in academic achievement compared to males (women now hold 61% of the MBAs and 50% of the doctorates in the U.S.). To me, this indicates that women are under-employed for their education and skill set, and/or expectations of women in the workplace are much higher than those for their male peers. The lack of objective performance-based pay makes it increasingly difficult for women's credentials and experience to hold the same weight as those of their male counterparts. It's hard to imagine that anyone would discount a women's degree from even a top institution, but it does happen.

Being Perceived as "Less"

As an IT executive in a large conglomerate, I was the most senior woman in my division for over five years, and the only woman to hold an MBA from a top-tier university. Most of the interactions with my male peers were cordial and professional, but every now and then perplexing behaviors from would pierce through those interactions. One day I was joking with several of my peers who had MBAs about where our respective alma maters ranked in Business Week's annual top B-school list, and one of my male peers—who didn't go to a top-ranked school, by the way—turned to me and said he was surprised I went to one of the top-ranked business schools. He also wanted to know what my test scores were, as if somehow a higher deity eliminated the entrance requirements just for me. For some reason, he didn't ask my peers that question.

After a pause, and a deep breath, I simply said that it was unfortunate he didn't make it into the school of his choice. There are bad and resentful behaviors in all organizations, and an occasional overt example of bias isn't necessarily indicative of a Club culture. However, when such behavior is the status quo, and it's condoned by the C-level team (that is, the top-ranking executives), you have to check in with yourself and your expectations about succeeding in that environment.

A notable study, "Orchestrating Impartiality: The Impact of 'Blind' Auditions on Female Musicians," conducted by Claudia Goldin and Cecilia Rouse,[7] exposed the biased perception against women's talents during their auditions for major orchestras. The authors investigated the increase in the number of women musicians as orchestras began adopting a blind audition process in the 1970s, allowing candidates to play behind a screen. Judges then made their decisions about who to advance to further rounds based on what they heard, rather than who they saw. The study found that blind auditions increased the probability that women would advance to further rounds of audition by 50%. During the 1970s, women represented 10% of the members of an orchestra, eventually climbing to 35% (at the New York Philharmonic) in 2000. The screen mattered a great deal regarding how the women's auditions were perceived by the male judges. Because the assessment process changed, women were able to compete against their male counterparts based on their skills and artistry rather than with the burden of their gender.

— □ —

...women can benefit by taking more control of their performance assessment.

— □ —

Another way I've seen performance assessments negatively impact women is in the simple act of human interaction. Some bosses just don't like giving appraisals, and won't do it because they are uncomfortable providing constructive criticism, or they are concerned about putting anything overly negative or positive in writing. Written performance assessments can be problematic when scrutinized by a legal team if the employee doesn't turn out to be the way he or she is depicted in an appraisal, so it's understandable that written assessments could pose some level of risk for a company. But this is where Club members gain an edge, in the informal and frequent communication with their boss and other decision-makers. They are receiving feedback on a more regular basis and have that fundamental opportunity to recalibrate well in advance of receiving their performance assessment, raise or bonus. This is an area where women can benefit from taking more control of their performance assessment by soliciting feedback directly from the person who controls their pay.

At one organization where I worked as a technology executive, it was understood that if you still had your job and you received an annual bonus you were doing fine. Club members, however, tend to overinflate the contributions of their teams and undervalue contributions by others, stacking the deck for promotions and Club membership in their favor. Without a fair-play, objective mechanism in place for assessing performance, women can expect to remain hampered in their quest to achieve parity with their male counterparts throughout their careers.

Clubs and Recognition

It's always interesting to me to read studies and conclusions about behavior that resonate with my professional experiences, particularly with regard to how women's contributions are recognized. In one notable research study conducted by Nancy Toder, several groups were asked to evaluate the work of men and women authors who wrote identical articles. One group was comprised of all men, another all women, and the final, a mix of men and women. The study concluded that in the presence of men, "both men and women devalued the female-authored articles" while women accorded men greater recognition and "preferential treatment." The preferential treatment ranged from "downgrading women, women's accomplishments, and the importance of interacting with women; by contrast, upgrading men and men's achievements, or deferring to men's leadership."[8]

Another study on jurors' participation during deliberation also uncovered disadvantages women face in being recognized as leaders. Men are typically selected as the foreperson or presiding juror on a jury, and have significantly higher participation rates during deliberation compared to women, making it difficult for women to shape the jury's deliberations.[9] Indeed, studies like this are applicable to women who are in a Club culture, because their ideas and solutions are routinely dismissed or devalued by Club members. I've heard numerous experiences from women whose peers — and sometimes clients — doubt their contributions, and even their qualifications, while never questioning those of their male counterparts. Several of the studies that confirm how women's qualifications are viewed compared to those of their male counterparts are discussed in Chapter 3, as an example of a lethal barrier to entry into a Club.

Another important point that resonates with my experience in relation to these studies is that most corporate decision-making occurs in meetings (and not by a silent vote), and if women are perceived as being of lower status and are not valued or heard in the same way as men when deliberating, it would negatively impact their ability to contribute what they know to the decision-making process and their ability to shape decisions.

Club Pressures Influence Outcomes

Club behavior goes beyond influencing decisions. It's not a stretch to say it *directs* group decisions, exerting pressure on non-members and creating repercussions for those who are not of like minds or who are deemed uncooperative. On several occasions, a peer of mine who was clearly a Club member would call me or stop in my office before an executive meeting, to talk about his ideas. He was quite proud of this tactic, which was to pre-deliberate with the other executives so that the "right" decision would be reached easily with the boss in the meeting room. He believed his own viewpoint was always the correct one, of course. I didn't know how much of his pre-deliberation and pre-meeting discussion took place with my other male peers, but I sensed that the other members probably already held views similar to his.

After a group meeting one day, this peer called one of my direct reports (a vice president-level member of my staff who reported directly to me), to provide his views on labor reporting and job scheduling, topics that were becoming increasingly rel-evant in the IT group. My staff member—who saw things through my lens as well as his own—stated, "I disagree with you!" The opinion rendered by my direct report was based on both his expertise with the IT group's project management systems and methodologies and his insider's view of the vastly divergent change requests coming from the management team. However, the repercussions for disagreeing with the Club member were immediate and quite painful for my direct report.

The Club member lambasted him until the conversation shut down, leaving him silent. Although the direct report was male, his gender had no relevance since he was viewed as an outsider, and guilty by association with me—another Club outsider.

– □ –

Recognizing Club behaviors and making a Club member aware of his or her bias...are the first steps in over-coming obstacles.

– □ –

After my direct report shared his experience with me, I stepped in and raised the issue with the Club member. Ultimately my peer apologized to both of us, saying that he didn't want to be that type of executive. The apology shed a positive light on the character of the Club member, but the incident begs examination on many levels. Such pressure and behavior eventually causes group members to silence themselves to avoid the negative consequences associated with disagreeing with people of influence,[10] and this in turn can lead to sub-optimal results for a company.

On an interpersonal level, I was surprised how effectively the situation was remedied just by pointing out the behavior to the Club member, who was not aware of how badly he impacted a valuable employee. Recognizing Club behaviors in your work environment and making a Club member aware of his or her bias or bad behavior are the first steps in overcoming obstacles and forging a successful career path for yourself.

I explore deep-seated biases further as another Lethal Barrier in Chapter 3, and in Chapter 6, I address the need to raise awareness of biases as a critical element of success.

Your Options

As an executive it may appear that you have only two courses of action against the pressures exerted by Club members: you can remain silent, withholding your opinions, facts and suggestions, or you can continue to provide your perspective regardless of the negative consequences. In reality though, it's not that clear-cut.

Your response will depend on your professional objectives and priorities for your area of responsibility and how comfortable you are with the risk of repercussions. Being perceived as a team player is an important factor for both genders, but the risks to your business, or your ability to deliver services, may outweigh the risks of disagreeing with a Club member as my direct report did above. It's much more difficult for female executives to weigh the risks of speaking out because they are already outside the Club. Saying "you have to pick your battles," or "lose a battle to win the war" is not a new or innovative idea. What is more compelling, and in hindsight more meaningful, is to discuss how you can effectively get your ideas heard as a woman in a Club environment without being perceived as the 'odd person out.' In Chapter 6, I suggest ways for avoiding the tendency to remain silent, and for getting comfortable with expressing a contrary view.

CHAPTER 1:

Summary Points

☐ All clubs require conformance to a set of beliefs and behaviors. It's when a 'club' crosses the threshold and becomes 'The Club' that women begin to experience startling behaviors and barriers in their careers.

☐ Negative aspects of The Club: Club-based organizations are exclusive and typically limit ideas, information flow and rewards to a select few. Club members calibrate to each other, not necessarily to the company's goals.

☐ Positive aspects of a club: Organizations that are team-based are inclusive and provide opportunities and access to ideas and people across the organization.

☐ Talent and drive aren't enough: Feeling excluded? Trust your gut. If it's telling you something isn't right, it probably isn't. Work doesn't need to be that difficult and unproductive. Team-based organizations can launch rocket ships, and your career.

☐ Assessing performance: Know how you will be evaluated and ask for feedback from the person who controls your pay.

☐ Being perceived as less: Club members gain an edge in the informal and frequent communication with their boss and other decision-makers. They have more opportunity to recalibrate well in advance of receiving their performance assessment, raise or bonus.

☐ Clubs and recognition: Studies show that women's ideas and accomplishments are not valued in the same way as their male peers. This negatively impacts their ability to contribute what they know to the decision-making process and their ability to shape decisions.

☐ Club pressures influence outcomes: Club behavior directs group decisions and exerts pressure on non-members to remain silent to avoid repercussions or appearing uncooperative.

CHAPTER 2:

Gender and Cultural Context

AS WOMEN MOVE UP THE CORPORATE ladder, a feeling of isolation often takes hold. This is, in part, because
women are held to different standards then men and are not
always supported by the people they have brought along with
them, including the women they have hired or promoted.
I attribute this not only to deep-rooted gender biases in
both men and women but to intense competition for senior
executive positions. This is probably the case for any corporate

executive, but women will have a smaller safety net or circle of confidants to support them.

Although isolation is a result of the corporate culture as well as social culture, I have found that it is more common for women executives to feel isolated because they are not socialized in the ways men are. For example, rarely will women be the recipient of NBA or MLB tickets in the company's suite. (This assertion is based on 30-plus years of personal experience as well as anecdotes from my female colleagues.) For those women and few men who have not yet embraced basketball, baseball, football, or hockey, it doesn't hurt to add a few applications to your mobile phone or bookmark the URLs of several major sports teams so you can become comfortable in sports-related conversations with your male peers. As long as there is a sincere interest, it may break down a few communication barriers. However, although such communication is an important part of developing rapport with a male-dominated Club in the workplace, don't expect it to be more than an ice breaker. It takes a great deal more to get men comfortable working with and for women. Women's experiences in the workplace remain vastly different from those of their male counterparts, and thus their points of view and perceptions also differ.

Gender Differences in the Workplace

These different perceptions lead to different inquiries and conclusions. For example, as I was evaluating outsourcers for an IT cost reduction initiative in 2008, my project team set up a conference call with one of the current customers of an outsourcer based in India. The executive who ran the customer's project management office (PMO) was a woman, and I asked her if she felt acknowledged as a management leader by the outsourcer they selected, given that she was working with an Indian culture not used to having a woman boss per se. She told me that the outsourcer recognized that she would be an important customer, and as a key decision-maker would have a say in evaluating their performance, which influenced how well they interacted with her. She then added that she was advocating for more women on the outsourcer's management team, knowing that women were not commonly placed in leadership roles in Indian firms. From my perspective, there was no ambiguity regarding the experience this female executive had managing an Indian outsourcing firm, and how I could apply her knowledge to my experience.

Interestingly, my question caused an immediate backlash from one of the male consultants in the advisory firm that my company had hired to help us with our due diligence process. The consultant sent me an email saying that I was culturally biased and that any concerns I may have had about gender disparity were unfounded. My response to this consultant was "as the highest-ranking woman in our organization, if I don't raise these questions, no one will." I realized at that moment that my male peers and leaders did not have the perspectives and experiences that only I could have as a woman. I certainly believed that all of the outsourcing firms had great people, but no one but me seemed to notice the obvious lack of women in the room.

I remember forwarding the email exchange I had with the consultant to the executive project leader in my company, with a comment about how isolating it was to be the lone woman in senior IT management, and the lone person bringing these perspectives to our selection committee. Although it wouldn't be a factor in selecting our outsourcing vendor, the executive project leader apologized for the lack of awareness on the consultant's part and subsequently reassigned him to another role.

Women's Roles within a Culture

The context of a woman's role within a culture directly correlates to how women are accepted and perceived in the workforce by that culture. This is the voice of experience speaking here, and although it is my voice, it reflects experiences of many women business executives I have worked with over the last three decades. In my previous example about evaluating outsourcing firms, I had a great opportunity to meet with several executive teams from leading global firms. One of the firms arranged a meeting with me and my team to have a more in-depth discussion regarding our IT responsibilities and expertise.

I came to the meeting with the head of my security team and one of his staff, and as we entered the room, several executives from the outsourcing firm ran over to the head of my security team to introduce themselves. They assumed he was the lead executive from my company. Graciously the security head turned to the outsourcing executives and said, "Let me introduce you to my boss." They were quite startled and of course very apologetic.

Not surprisingly, the outsourcing company had no women executives, or at least none that were present during that meeting. The few women who did accompany them were "manning" the laptops and PowerPoint presentations. While this wasn't a common occurrence in my career, it does illustrate an experience that a man would never encounter. If I were a man, someone from the global firm would have naturally asked about the reporting structure. Because I was a female, the assumption was made at the onset that I was not the person in charge. Was this the result of an overt bias, or was there another explanation for these behaviors?

Bias or Heuristics?

Dr. Christopher Hsee (Professor of Behavioral Science at the University of Chicago Booth School) and I have discussed the above scenario. His view is that it makes sense for people to make a decision based on heuristics—in this case, what they have encountered in the past. It's possible that in the outsourcing company's experience, it wasn't the 'average' occurrence for a woman to be in charge of the security function, and based on the average experience, assuming that a man was in charge of that technology function was actually in the executives' favor.

$-\square-$

cultural norms...create

powerful references and perceptions.

$-\square-$

I agree that cultural norms with regard to women's roles create powerful references and perceptions. Although Dr. Hsee's explanation is more plausible to me in the context of an earlier century, it gives credence to the power of heuristics, which builds over time and frame women's roles in any culture.

One of the most memorable experiences I had confronting perceptions of women in a societal context came on a flight to Hong Kong. I was on my way to see a client and was on the plane stowing my luggage like everyone else around me. I was flying out of Denver and had at least a 12-hour flight ahead of me, which was plenty of time to prepare for my first meeting. While I was hoisting a few items into the overhead bin, a gentleman tapped me on the shoulder and asked if I would hang his coat up. He assumed I was a flight attendant! (I politely declined to hang his coat up.) If I view that experience through a heuristic lens, I'm inclined to conclude that I was mistaken for a flight attendant because (a), I was dressed in business attire, and (b) there were very few women flying in business class. Regardless of the rationalization, it still felt like a bias to me.

In another example, the organizational hierarchy was determined prior to our business meetings. In 2004, I traveled to Japan to meet with the chief design executives of all of the leading auto manufacturers. The auto companies arranged the seating so that the president of my organization would sit at the center of the table, and I would sit to the right of him, signaling that I was the next-highest-ranking executive. The hosting auto companies would align their executives across the table from us, matching rank accordingly. Although my stature as a business person was clear to everyone during the meeting, I was still the last one served tea in the room—because of my gender. After the meeting, only the men were asked to stay behind for drinks and further conversation. Again, it can be argued that heuristics guided the other attendees' perceptions, but bias remains a possibility.

Have the Times Changed?

As a participant in the Executive in Residence Program at the University of Chicago Booth School of Business, I had the wonderful opportunity to mentor a dozen or so students over a winter weekend in Chicago. This particular weekend was very cold, windy and wet. I was impressed with the students' unwavering desire to meet with an alumna/experienced management practitioner during such a cold weekend, and with their general intensity and passion for business. The young women who attended my sessions had already racked up some remarkable accomplishments, yet they all expressed career concerns with a common theme of feeling isolated by their male peers. The isolation was described in various ways and included the sports-centered conversations I mentioned earlier. One woman in particular stood out because she was a highly educated engineer who spoke several languages, yet she was excluded from lunches with her male peers—who also happened to have easier access to her boss. She was bewildered by The Club behavior and professionally stymied by it. She was looking for ways to increase her comfort level in her work environment, as well as increase the comfort level of her peers.

As I discuss in Chapter 6, my first suggestion was for her to start building rapport with one person on the team and with her boss, and continue from there. Who could have imagined that women would continue to struggle for acceptance from their male peers in the American workplace in the 21st century?

CHAPTER 2:

Summary Points

☐ Becoming comfortable with sports-talk may break down a few communication barriers, as long as it's sincere, but women are still responsible for making men comfortable with their presence.

☐ Women have work experiences that are unique to their gender; men will never be mistaken for a flight attendant or someone's assistant when they are the boss.

☐ Both bias and heuristics contribute to beliefs about women's leadership capabilities based on their cultural context.

CHAPTER 3:

Club Behaviors –
Lethal Barriers to Entry and What to do to Meet the Challenge

BEING AWARE OF THE LETHAL BARRIERS to entry into The Club is the first step in assessing your organization, peer interactions and your contributions (particularly how your contributions may be perceived in your organization). I've distilled 30 years of experience observing and working in several Club-based organizations into the Club behaviors and cultural norms that constitute the barriers that have a significant impact on a woman's career progression. These are also the behaviors that the many women I've known and worked with over the years experienced themselves. These behaviors can emanate from your peers, your boss, or other executives with whom you routinely interact.

Not only are these behaviors detrimental to your career and personal satisfaction, they are behaviors that are most detrimental to a company's performance and shareholders. They are also the most palpable because they are observable behaviors that can be tested and validated, which will in turn help you make the right decisions for you and your organization. Regularly checking your work environment against the Lethal Barriers to Entry can keep you focused on your goals while you take the steps to forge a successful career path.

Organizations, and people in those organizations, may exhibit some of the Lethal Barriers to Entry behaviors from time to time, but it may not be indicative of a true Club culture. The way to tease it out is by looking at behavioral patterns and the frequency of the behaviors that impact you as well as other woman executives. All of the barriers are addressable and require action on your part. Each barrier described below is followed by real examples of what you can do to successfully navigate your career and achieve your potential. Keep in mind that Barrier awareness is about you in relation to the company you are working in, and in relation to your career goals. Individual experiences with a company will vary, but it's your interaction with the overarching cultural environment that requires scrutiny.

Lethal Barriers to Entry

1. Intimidation Tactics: Bullies Rule
2. Deep-rooted Biases
3. In the Audience, Not on the Stage: Where the Opportunities Are, and Who Gets Them
4. Budget Control
5. Resistance
6. Double Standards

Intimidation Tactics: Bullies Rule

We all know how harmful a bully can be to you and your peer group; the behavior first seen in grade school, bullying can carry on through middle school and high school, and then on to adulthood when it's unchecked. When bullying behavior is evident in a corporate environment, it is always a reflection of the top leadership of that organization and the culture they have created. Club-type behavior fosters corporate bullying, meaning that your work ethics, decisions, output, and strategies will be challenged on all fronts by The Club members if they disagree with your convictions.

This is usually the case because you are the outsider and will present divergent opinions and approaches. This particular behavior, far more than the others discussed in this book, is experienced equally across males and females who are not part of The Club, though it is much harder for women to combat these behaviors in the workplace

A male peer with whom I worked for several years at a large conglomerate, and who was not in The Club, referred to his

47

bullying experience as "hazing." He inherited the challenging task of overseeing a project that required collaboration from the Club since they would be sharing the same technology environment. The Club wanted my peer to adopt their methodology and time tables, which wasn't suitable to the business unit he was supporting. The business unit had revenue streams and distribution channel constraints, and as my peer quickly realized, he had no influence over the Club's insistence on doing it their way. After all, the Club had worked a certain way in the past, and to them it was the only way to proceed.

My peer was challenged by Club members at every phase of the project, and put in excruciatingly long hours to continually reassure everyone that the project status was not flawed, the quality of the work was adequate, and basically that there was a low risk of impacting users of his business unit's global system. It turned out he had been besieged by what appeared to be rather civil, mannered executives. However, that was on the surface. The real conflict occurred behind the scenes, with the Club members lobbying their clients and other executives with what they referred to as "their intelligence" and "inside information" about the project, casting doubt that the executive was competent and perpetually raising issues about the viability of the project going live. The Club culture made the experience quite painful and unnecessarily time-consuming. However, my peer successfully launched his project to the acclaim of the business unit he supported, and he continued to work alongside the Club quite well for several years, until he chose to leave the company for a better opportunity.

When "Passion" Is Aggression

Another more common experience of bullying is in the form of plain old aggression. One of my executive-level employees told me on several occasions that the reason he was so loud and animated in meetings was because he was passionate about his opinions and about the work of his team. He viewed his behavior as a committed campaign for his principles and the quality of his work. For most women, behavior that is loud, animated and aggressive looks, sounds, and feels like aggression, even when it's not directed at you. It's often impossible to tell the difference between someone's passion and aggression. Do I expect everyone to agree with their colleagues on every point and then hold hands and sing around a campfire? No, but I expect executives to articulate their thoughts and opinions to both their seniors and peers in the best possible manner for them to be understood and evaluated against other ideas, and in a manner that conveys character and simple respect. Otherwise they should try another career path.

— □ —

Club cultures tend to...
fuel aggressive behaviors.

— □ —

Unfortunately, Club cultures tend to condone and even fuel aggressive behavior and then pass it off as a sign of strength, which some women have begun to emulate. Over the years I've confronted many instances of bullying behavior, and in almost all cases, the bullies were aware of it; in some cases, they had a record of histrionics and yet the company accepted the behavior as the status quo. This is a fundamental detriment of Club behavior. The most talented, driven, hard-working individuals may be blocked from top positions in a Club-based organization because opportunities for advancement are given to a select few who pattern their behaviors after that of other Club members.

Companies that put up the Barriers to Entry may be quite successful financially and have no need to change in this regard. Shareholders don't see the bullying behavior, and they don't care about the company's culture unless the company isn't meeting their performance goals.

The Board of Directors' Influence

However, the board of directors—particularly the compensation committee—should be asking about the executive placement process to insure the company is attracting and more importantly promoting the best talent within the company. I had a rare opportunity to meet with one of the most senior managers in my division whom many people speculated was a strong influencer in The Club. We were briefing him on some of the property rights management studies and assumptions with a consultant. During the meeting, there were diverging opinions about what data the business units would want to manage versus a centralized corporate approach. At one point, the senior executive got up and threw the presentation deck at the presenter, made a disparaging remark and left the room. There were a few other Club members in the room and when

I later asked one of them about what happened, he said he had never seen that before. Over the years however, several people had shared their stories about how commonplace these experiences were with this senior leader. Depending on your proximity to The Club, the perception and acceptance of the bullying behavior will vary.

What you can do:

Bullying by a Club member, or by the entire Club, is an observable occurrence. You have to ask yourself whether the bullying type behavior of the Club is systemic enough or harmful enough for you to take action. By taking action I mean discussing the events with your HR and legal team, someone on the senior management team or the CEO, leaving the organization, or accepting the environment for what it is and potentially minimizing contact with the worst offenders (the latter option is detrimental to the company and shareholders as it minimizes productivity). In the cases where you have some influence over the bully, you can make headway by raising his or her awareness and the company's awareness of the behavior. Regardless of the size of the organization you are working in, without the support from your company's leadership team to stop the bullying behavior, you won't get very far. One woman executive who worked in a financial services company was told to "get over it" when she reluctantly reported bullying behavior to her senior manager. She decided to leave the company and found another where her contributions were recognized and whose culture was more supportive of a diverse group of people.

Embedded Behavior

However, if the bully happens to be the Club leader, it's likely the behavior is embedded in the culture. In one company, I had a peer who had a habit of taking a pen and pointing it at a person's face when he wanted to make a point (okay, it was more like thrusting it in your face). He did this equally to men and women, and it seemed to go unnoticed by the men in the room. I asked one of the few female executives after a meeting if she noticed the pen thrusting since it made me uncomfortable, and she declared that she would never meet with that executive alone because of this behavior. To a woman, that gesture looks and feels like aggression. To a Club member, it goes unchallenged.

That female executive left the company after a very brief period, but she successfully leveraged her experience and went on to a Chief Information Officer position with a competitor where she was readily accepted on the senior management team. Although leaving your company and position is always an option, it may not be the right option for your career goals, and it should be considered against other opportunities. It turns out that a number of people came forth and discussed the male executive's pen thrusting conduct (among other behaviors) with the HR team and his boss, and within about 18 months, the male executive moved on to another company. So, change can occur if you take the right steps and consider all of your options.

Flagrant Bullying

Egregious bullying requires a different course. If behavior exceeds what one would expect from a heated debate over business issues, formal and swift action is required. Most large companies have a compliance officer and senior HR executive who will guide you through the process of filing a report and keeping you above the ensuing fray. Fortunately, I have experienced full-on, overt bullying only once in my management career.

I had been a manager for about 10 years at the time when the bullying occurred. It started in a company meeting that I attended with another woman and a male sales support staff member. He had a reputation of calling the shots and being his own boss, and was pretty much known for having a lot of leeway to conduct his business. Someone on the sales team was always trying to track him down because he and his crew had such flexible work hours. Going into the meeting, the other woman and I knew that the sales support person wanted to address some issues, and we expected the conversation to be intense. However, we couldn't have anticipated the escalating behavior that took hold of him once the door closed. He proceeded to accuse us of discrediting him with his boss, and he repeatedly screamed "don't ever speak to my boss again" while slamming his fist on the table. He had a few other choice words for us, but we remained calm and tried to assure him he must be mistaken, but his behavior kept escalating.

I was the first one to leave the room when his screaming overtook any hope for dialogue. When I left, I simply walked back to my office and closed the door in disbelief, trying to replay what had happened. I didn't think I could or should do anything. I had taken some lumps and it wasn't pleasant, and I was reflecting on what I could have done to control the outcome of the meeting when the phone rang. It was the head of HR asking if I was alright. A co-worker whose office was near the conference room called HR when the screaming began. It was so loud it could be heard down the hall through closed doors.

By the time I had walked back to my office, they had already taken swift action to stop the escalation. The company then looked to this employee's senior manager to take immediate steps to correct and prevent the bullying behavior. He was eventually managed out of the organization. This experience was an invaluable reminder that women must take charge, empower themselves, and call attention to bad behaviors in Club-based organizations in order to effect changes.

Deep-rooted Biases

Most men are not aware of how deeply rooted their biases are against women in the workplace. Women are expected to act and dress according to the social standards for a female, making it difficult to shift their social context so their male peers can perceive them, and more importantly accept them, as effective leaders. A more technical way of describing the expectations of the male and female persona in the workplace is based on what Dr. Kristen Schilt, an assistant professor of sociology at the University of Chicago, refers to in her book, "Just One of the Guys?: Transgender Men and the Persistence of Inequality,"[11] as the "institutionalization of the male/female binary" which "relies more on the logic of culture than on the science of chromosomes."

Due to the "logic of culture," most women try to make work interactions with male peers cordial and collaborative at the onset, but inevitably, biases often present themselves in unexpected ways. I have managed hundreds of male and female employees, and I have worked for dozens of men and women.

Personally I wasn't prepared for the obstacles women endure to gain equal footing on the executive team, or the negative impact these biases have on women's career development and status within their organizations. I just assumed that if I worked hard and delivered on my boss's and customer's expectations I would succeed.

– □ –

...*women continue to face hiring and promotion discrimination.*

– □ –

To a large degree that proved fruitful for me, as well as for many other woman leaders that I have interviewed, but it was also obvious that I was routinely clocking in earlier and staying later than most of my male colleagues. The idea that women continue to face hiring and promotion discrimination in the 21st century seems implausible to some degree, especially for companies that tout their diversity programs (while maintaining a Club culture).

A Look at Gender Statistics

As a 'category' of workers, women haven't made much progress in ascending to the most senior ranks in corporations, which ultimately affects their chances of being selected for board positions, and it is necessary to explore the statistical impact of these biases.

According to the "2010 Board of Directors Survey" published by Heidrick & Struggles,[12] women have a longer and harder path to the boardroom compared to men. Women in the survey reported taking 1.75 times longer to land their first board position (28 months for women vs. 16 months for men). Women also felt stronger about the need for boards to actively promote diversity compared to their male counterparts (62% of women vs. 43% of men reported feeling this way).

Strikingly, a significant percentage of women board members believed they brought special attributes to a board, in stark contrast to the opinions of their male counterparts (90% of women vs. 56% of men). Women want to be viewed as having special attributes, which in turn adds value to a company and board, although it's not clear what the special attributes are that one gender brings to the table over the other. Neither group 'agreed' or 'strongly agreed' with imposing quotas on boards. It's interesting that companies and boards don't want to impose quotas given that so little progress has been made in promoting women.

– □ –

...deep-rooted biases can completely

block opportunities for women,

starting with the recruitment process.

– □ –

Men still make the majority of hiring decisions, and without 'encouragement' they will continue to hire candidates they are most comfortable with no matter how unintentional the biased behavior becomes in the organization. Other countries (e.g., Norway and Spain) have already introduced quotas that require boards to fill 40% of their seats with women.[13] Italy,

France and Belgium are also considering similar interventions, but whether a capitalism-based U.S. economic structure that promotes free markets and competition will adopt such a standard remains to be seen. Some intervention is clearly needed to break through the barriers.

More Hoops and Hurdles

Jumping through more hoops than a man to be acknowledged, accepted, or rewarded as a woman executive in a Club culture is more the norm than the exception. When it comes to career development, deep-rooted biases can completely block opportunities for women, starting with the recruitment process. Unless someone asks a company recruiter to provide a diverse set of candidates for review, there is a high probability that you won't see many resumes from qualified women. Many resumes are discounted before the hiring manager has had a chance to review them. If they do pass the recruiter, and the hiring manager is male, it is also likely the resume will be discounted in some way that the hiring manager may not even be aware of.

One male executive I worked with for several years had a habit of saying "she doesn't have to work" whenever he interviewed a potential female candidate who was married. One day I asked him what he meant by using that phrase when he came upon a married candidate, and he said that as long as the candidate was married, she could fall back on her spouse's income when she got tired of working, and therefore the woman didn't really need to work. In other words, the married woman's resume would be discounted and placed in a lower hiring status because he believed she didn't really need the job, or she didn't have the motivation to work as hard as her male counterparts. I found this troubling but at the same time recognized that this male executive from all other aspects of his work was very respectful and supportive of women. His deep biases, however, were clearly influencing his hiring decisions.

Biases in Both Genders

A 1999 study called "The Impact of Gender on the Review of the Curricula Vitae of Job Applicants and Tenure Candidates"[14] calls attention to this behavior. The study examined 238 male and female academic psychologists, and found that both the men and women evaluated resumes with a male name much more positively than resumes with a female name even though the resumes were virtually identical in terms of education, experience, and publications. The fact that both genders are socialized to interpret the contributions of a male as more valuable than a female who has similar or even identical achievements makes the road to leadership that much harder for women; hence the nagging feeling that women have to work harder is actually fueled by fact.

Dr. Kristen Schilt has teased out remarkable gender biases in her work with transgender men. In her studies, she found that men who transitioned to being female did not have the opportunities for advancement they previously had as males, earning 32% less after they transitioned from male to female, while females who transitioned to males found they were more accepted and more successful as males.[15] In studying many aspects of transgender career goals, education, and pay both prior to the gender change and post-gender change, Dr. Schilt further uncovered the grim reality of gender biases in the workplace.

The Saga of the Golf Cart

What appears to be collegial behavior on the surface may in fact mask the underpinnings of a Club-based culture. This brings me to my golf cart saga. It was common for executives at my level to have a golf cart to use around the company campus to save time commuting from one meeting to another. The campus was quite large, and in-person meetings were often scheduled back-to-back. From a productivity perspective, it made sense to enable the availability of the executive team by providing them with some means of transportation. After a few months establishing myself in my position, I asked my boss for a golf cart.

He directed me to a male peer who managed both the infrastructure team and the fleet of golf carts for our division. My boss didn't want to purchase a new cart without exploring the use of the current fleet. The approach seemed fair to me. So far so good, right? Of course not! I met with my peer in his office, which had a large window overlooking the parking area where at least six carts were idly parked in their spaces. Obviously the carts were not being used, and I naively thought that this would play in my favor. Wrong. My peer told me that he couldn't give up a cart because he needed them "for the technicians," just in case they got a service call and had to run equipment across the campus to make a quick repair. Being a data-minded person, I asked how often the carts were actually in use, since he mentioned that the carts were shared among the technicians; one of the administrative assistants handed out the keys as needed. Interestingly, he didn't have that data. His group was busy, he contended, and they weren't tracking the carts' usage. My peer was adamant—he couldn't spare a cart for me.

I'd never thought that I would be obliged to compete against technicians, who could easily walk to their destinations and who rarely carried more than a cable or hard drive with them. It was clear that my status wasn't considered as valuable as that of the technicians, or even in the same way as my other male peers, who appeared to have easy access to carts. So, I went back to my boss with a plea to purchase a new cart because all of the current carts needed to be available for technicians.

Surprisingly, my boss didn't buy the rationale I had been given. He called my peer and said "give her a cart." After all, he was my peer's boss and could influence the outcome. A perfect outcome, right? Not so fast. I did get a cart, but it was the worst cart in the fleet. The seats were torn out of the back. A flat bed had been added to it at some point to haul things around. The brakes and lights didn't work, and the electric cable was thrown in the back because the recoiling mechanism was broken.

It took several thousand dollars of my budget and about a month's worth of work to restore the cart to its full potential (thanks to my very savvy assistant). In the end, the hurdles weren't insurmountable, but they were a distraction from more meaningful work, and for that, the company suffered in the end. My department name was eventually added to the windshield, and for good measure I glued a can of paper-mâché flowers in the cup holder which my artist friend gave me to celebrate the "taking of the cart." Not surprisingly, very few of my male peers wanted to borrow the cart with those lovely, bright flowers in them.

Cinderella Syndrome

Club environments can also confine women to lower-level positions by taking advantage of their work ethic and lack of power; by this I mean the realities of handling two or more times the workload of their counterparts, or handling an equal load with less support. I refer to this as the Cinderella Syndrome, because the unpleasant side of that classic fairytale illustrates how it feels to be the 'outsider' expected to work tirelessly supporting others, with few resources. One of my University of Chicago Booth graduate school alumnae who was also one of my business colleagues during my consulting years worked diligently and conscientiously for a top Fortune 100 technology company for over five years. She eventually left to start her own consulting firm, which proved to be not only a better work/life fit while she was raising her two children, but also more lucrative than her corporate job, enabling her to pay for her children's education. She was married with a working spouse, but her desire to work was similar to that of many educated, professional women. She wanted a good life for her family, wanted to be a role model for her children, and wanted to contribute to the GDP in the true spirit of someone holding an MBA from a top institution.

While still working at her corporate job, she noticed that all of the corner offices were occupied by men, and all of the offices in between were occupied by women. When she approached one of the executives and pointed this out, he willingly offered that he "prefers to hire women because they work harder than men." But what about the women's career path to the corner offices? He never thought to address the fundamental issue behind her observation. Women do work harder than men because we have to jump through more hoops to reach our goals, and because we are locked out of the informal networking and mentoring that takes place in Club cultures. However, the "hard-working woman" bias can work against woman because they tend to remain in positions that require them to over-work and lose opportunities for growth.

Michele V. Gee and Sue Margaret Norton from the University of Wisconsin-Parkside co-authored a paper titled "Improving the Status of Women in the Academy."[16] They cite the tendency for academic organizations to burden women academics with "excessive service commitments" such as student orientation, which is not valued in the decision-making process when it comes time to award tenure or full professorships. The same rings true in the corporate world when women are asked to absorb work and problems from areas outside their core responsibilities. In one company I worked for, we called these additional service commitments "extra-credit assignments." They ranged from coordinating facility moves to soliciting donations. Although men were asked to take on these assignments as well, they were more comfortable saying "no." For the women executives who felt pressure to accept the assignments, the result was usually negative in that valuable time was redirected away from the strategic aspects of their roles.

What you can do:

Now that you're armed with the facts and real-life stories, what can you do to reduce the deep-rooted bias barrier? The best way to unseat gender biases from an individual or an organization is to confront them head-on. I realize that this idea will make many readers cringe because it once again places women in an adversarial role and unfairly makes them "persona non grata" with their employers and peers.

– □ –

...without women speaking up...the Club behavior will continue to thrive.

– □ –

However, without women speaking up—which can be done without being confrontational —and starting the discussion on gender issues, the Club behavior will continue to thrive. Becoming a champion for diversity and the benefits diversity brings to your organization is a good place to start, by giving your peers and the management team insight into women's experiences, as well as the practices that may be limiting your company's potential.

Start the Dialogue

Mary Lou Schmidt, MD, Associate Professor and Head of the Pediatric Hematology and Oncology Division, College of Medicine at the University of Illinois, and co-author with Claudia Morrissey, MD, of "Fixing the System, Not the Women: An Innovative Approach to Faculty Advancement,"[17] shared with me that one of the most effective steps toward defeating bias is to start the dialogue with the leadership of your organization, armed of course with data. She found that a bit of humor helped the leadership's absorption of the data. Here in Chapter 4 ("It Starts at the Top"), I discuss in greater detail her journey and the challenges that influenced change at the leadership levels at the University of Illinois Medical College.

The fact that women continue to face employment discrimination in the 21st century seems implausible to some degree, especially when companies that tout their diversity programs maintain a Club culture unfavorable to women. Walmart appears to be the reference point as one of those companies. They established an Office of Diversity in 2003 to focus on "fostering a high-performance culture based on inclusion," "giving every associate the opportunity to learn, grow and advance."[18] So let's consider the gender discrimination class action suit filed against Walmart in 2001 on behalf of all past and present female associates (up to 1.5 million women), claiming that Walmart paid its female employees lower wages and gave them fewer promotions than men, even when the women had better performance reviews and higher seniority than their male counterparts.

Although women represent 70% of Walmart's hourly employees, men represent 86% of its 3,400 store managers. Clearly their talent pipeline is stocked with women. I doubt you'll find that Walmart would admit to hiring women who were not "promotable," since it would contradict their elegant articulation of opportunity and advancement.

However, Walmart follows common business practices, allowing its managers to make hiring decisions. If the majority of the managers are men, should we be surprised that they are promoting men? What's even more disturbing than the facts is that in June 2011 the U.S. Supreme Court justices rendered a 5 to 4 split decision (along gender lines) that the suit could not proceed as a class action suit. Those Justices that clearly saw Walmart's behavior as obvious discrimination were the women: Justices Ruth Bader Ginsberg, Sonia Sotomayor and Elena Kagan,[19] while five of the six male Justices saw things differently.

Justice Ginsberg's dissenting opinion reflected on how gender bias "suffused" Walmart's culture. In contrast, Justice Antonin Scalia contended that the women claiming gender discrimination didn't prove enough. He saw Walmart's policy of allowing its managers to make hiring and promotion decisions for their stores as merely an exercise in discretion. One wonders, can anyone reasonably believe that a company would have to explicitly state that their hiring policy says *not* to promote women for discrimination to exist?[20]

Walmart's management practices, supported by the data, show otherwise. It would appear that company policies are not enough to prevent gender biases without external, third party oversight. To me the finer point is the pay and promotion data that were ignored by the male Justices. They didn't see it as proof, and yet these data are the strongest indicator of gender bias that exists in corporate cultures. One wonders whether the Supreme Court's decision would have been different if the pay and promotion data showed that men were under-represented in the management ranks.

"Group Think"

The Supreme Court's decision is reminiscent of the flawed conclusions made in 1979 by the supervisors and operators of the Three Mile Island nuclear reactor when they disregarded the readings from the reactor's primary monitoring devices and instead relied on a secondary indicator tracking the power to the pilot-operated relief valve (PORV) prior to the meltdown.[21] Erroneous decisions were made when the primary indicators and data were ignored or overlooked. Many behavioral scientists refer to the Three Mile Island meltdown as a prime example of "group think," because of the operators' group-reinforced belief that the absence of the PORV indicator light was a better signal than the other monitoring devices at their disposal. It would seem that even U.S. Supreme Court Justices can be challenged by their group biases.

Later in this book I recommend more assertive remedies, but fundamentally women must start using labor statistics to support their viewpoints and start raising the issues with their senior management teams. Women have been too quiet for too long because we've been working hard to be accepted by our male peers and are reluctant to rock the boat. Unfortunately, we lost an opportunity to alter Club culture and gain traction in senior positions and in the boardroom because we haven't gained critical mass, and when we do reach the executive levels of a corporation or in leadership positions in academia, we remain socially segregated.

– □ –

...the fallback position will be to seek opportunities in companies that will support your aspirations.

– □ –

As Rosabeth Moss Kanter points out, "Numbers, proportional representation, are important not only because they symbolize the presence or absence of discrimination but also because they have real consequences for performance."

She notes that the performance consequences of the few number of women in senior management and on boards is to "overcompensate through either achievement or hiding successes, or to turn against people of his or her kind." [22]

Some companies have successfully built strong non-biased cultures, and women need to encourage their own companies to follow suit. I interviewed a female senior executive from IBM who has been with the company on and off since 1977, and she praised the company for building a culture where her accomplishments were recognized and her ideas were heard throughout her career. She credits IBM with building a culture that is very supportive of women, particularly citing the mentorship program that is part of every executive's obligation to the company. In such an environment, she was able to freely discuss her career aspirations and take on responsibilities and roles that led her to her goal. She was one of the few women I have interviewed who said she had not faced any biases or Club-based challenges in her career. If you are in a biased culture, and you cannot raise awareness or influence change, then the fallback position will be to seek opportunities in companies that *will* support your aspirations.

In terms of absorbing more work that leads to nowhere, we have to become comfortable saying "no, unless I have x" or "yes, but only if I have y."

In the Audience, Not on the Stage: Where the Opportunities Are, and Who Gets Them

My roommate from undergraduate school came into Los Angeles to celebrate the 17th anniversary of the touring company of Phantom of the Opera. We were both music majors as undergraduates. She went into music as a career while I went on to pursue Cobol and BASIC programming along with structured systems design and wireless data technologies. She was in the cast of the touring company and thought it would be fun to meet for lunch and catch up on our careers. We talked about our "badges" of success and how hard we worked to achieve a certain status in our careers, and she described how The Club works in her world.

In a theatrical cast, you are either in a lead role or a non-lead, supporting role. Leads hang out with other leads and rarely give the non-leads a nod. On occasion, a lead would cross over the line and include the non-leads in conversation or a social setting. This wasn't the unusual part, since organizational hierarchies exist everywhere and one's professional sphere of contacts changes as one's career progresses. The chord that resonated with me was the understanding that my friend's role as a guest when invited to lunch or a party with the lead cast members was to be their audience—frequent affirmation and accolades were expected. Playing the role of audience member does not get you into The Club, but it allows you to be juxtaposed to it.

This is one of the attributes of Club behavior. Non-Club members get to be the audience. Over the course of several years at a company where I was a senior-level IT executive, I facilitated regular meetings with my boss and other senior executives, spending hours with my staff compiling data and incorporating status updates from my peers for review by the management committee. By anyone's measurement, that was a lot of interaction with the same group of people, and yet the conversation was typically unilateral.

In the corporate world, many decisions are reached through group deliberations, and it's common for individuals who are not part of the "in crowd" to silence themselves when they hold an opinion different from that of the group and they don't want to suffer the consequences of expressing a dissenting opinion, or they just don't want to be scrutinized even if they agree with what is being said. It's quite possible to be included in the deliberation process as an "audience member," to add a sense of support to the decisions in the way my college roommate was included to provide affirmation to the leading actors in the cast. In another setting, a Department Chair from a leading medical college compared her experiences as an audience member to the role of bystander or cheerleader on a professional sports team, where she was expected to support her male colleagues, but wasn't invited to play on the field.

— □ —

*...women carry the responsibility
(or burden) of making men
comfortable with their presence.*

— □ —

What you can do:

Breakthroughs do occur, and what worked for me was to engage one or two Club members with specific questions about them, or the business. I'm sure you've heard about the "30-second elevator speech" from executives and executive recruiters. The idea is to be prepared to concisely describe what you do and more importantly what your interests are when your opportune moment presents itself. While I'm an advocate of any technique that develops concise communication, I find the practical application of this quite challenging because it requires a willing and interested listener. What I have observed to be more successful during an audience "moment" is to ask questions about the Club's interests and expectations. In the end, women carry the responsibility (or burden) of making men comfortable with their presence. That can only happen if women accept the challenge and take the first steps to find common ground.

Be Prepared

For example, although I've worked for senior executives who insisted on frequent and lengthy meetings, most executives, including Club members, do not want to have meetings just for the sake of meeting. Getting clarification about your role in a meeting or on a project is critical. What do they specifically need from you, and what do they expect the output or results to look like? Then be prepared to say how you can and will contribute to the decision or process. As an audience member you may not be given a vote per se, but you want to pave the way for creating an environment where your data and opinions will be considered.

You also have to consider carefully what work is filling your plate and taking up your time. Using empirical data will help. What priorities command most of your attention and what are the time commitments for those priorities? How many projects do you oversee or how much revenue are you responsible for, and how much time is needed to insure a quality result? Having the answers will help you determine the value of special "opportunities." If you're asked to take on committee work, or sponsor a special interest group at work, you have to evaluate the opportunity in terms of how it will enhance your career or your personal goals; otherwise you won't have the time to pursue meaningful work that can lead you from a supporting role in the audience to a leading role on stage.

Budget and Resource Control

Budget disparity is one of the most lethal barriers to overcome, because it forces women to work longer and harder than their male counterparts and increases their risk of failure. Without adequate staff and funding, projects and services will result in less-than-optimal results no matter which gender is in charge. Throughout this chapter we've seen why women often face greater obstacles as business managers who need to acquire, and hold onto, the financial resources and headcount necessary to support their responsibilities and accomplish their goals. In Club-based organizations the opportunities, financial resources and staff are more easily directed to insiders and the trusted Club members, while women struggle with higher levels of scrutiny and resistance to their budget requests.

In one of the many capital budget meetings I've attended over the length of my career, one of my male peers stated that he needed at least $30 million to implement a project. He didn't provide any hourly estimates or project plans to justify that amount, as other non-members were required to do. In lieu of the usual grilling about priorities and rationale, he was only asked if he could do it for $25 million instead. The head of finance not only trusted this Club member, he was a personal advocate of the types of projects the Club member was given in the past.

However, everyone else who presented budget requests that day were expected to provide the standard business rationale, requirements, alternatives and return on investment calculations to the senior finance managers to justify their requests.

At another organization, I was awarded an ample budget to redesign the organization's web site and to evaluate, select and implement a new enterprise resource planning (ERP) system to support electronic commerce. Midway through the ERP evaluation, the President called me into his office and requested I donate a sizable portion of my budget to a special media project that one of his Club members would be leading. Although I made clear the negative impact the budget reduction would have on my project's outcome, I was still told to reduce my budget and complete my project as expected. Abandoning the project was not an option.

$-\square-$

...men and women still hold
on to beliefs that men should
command more.

$-\square-$

Unfortunately, men and women still hold on to beliefs that men should command more attention and authority when it comes to budget control. One woman director I interviewed held a doctorate in physical therapy, overseeing all aspects of a physical therapy program for a large state university. She worked mostly among other women, which was not unusual in this field. The ratio of women to men "bosses" in her organization was 5 to 1. Since women held the majority of leadership positions, she hadn't given much thought to gender bias. However, she was acutely aware that the few men at her level controlled more money and resources compared to the female bosses, and she felt that they garnered more attention from the university's administration because they were men. She speculated that the men's physical characteristics—being tall, or having a deep voice—may have had a dominating or even intimidating effect on the administration during budget discussions.

What you can do:

You can turn budget disparity into a positive result. Providing alternative outcomes based on funding levels is key to setting expectations when Club members control the budget. Linking expected outcomes (such as selecting an ERP system to accommodate all business requirements) to the business objectives will also clearly establish what is minimally required to fund a successful outcome. In the case where I was asked to reduce my budget to support a Club member's special project, I presented two alternatives to the President which compared system costs against different sets of business requirements. At the time, the organization was planning to expand internationally and wanted the new system to support multiple currencies. Without that requirement, lower-cost solutions became viable. In the end, the international requirement was dropped, and a new version of an existing ERP system became the right solution at a lower price point. I simply reframed the solution and expectations in light of the reduced budget.

Staying on top of work volumes, service levels, and head-count is critically important to supporting your requests for adequate resources to accomplish your business objectives. Although acquiring additional resources is easier for men and particularly for Club members, women can help themselves a great deal by relying on data to set expectations about what their budgets can realistically produce.

Resistance

Resistance manifests itself in many forms. My golf cart saga is one example of resistance, but there are other, subtler means of resistance by a Club that build up over time. Resistance can look and feel like a series of hurdles that athletes jump over in a competitive race. When resistance by the Club increases, it could be verging on an inhospitable or hostile environment, and you will have to weigh your experiences to determine whether you are experiencing only resistance or something much more serious.

In my experience, resistance is subtle but its effects have a significant impact. For example, I interviewed a woman who works for a prestigious university in California; she has had a long and quite successful tenure with the institution as a Program Director. As the management team started to change in her organization, she began to notice that everyday operational processes that were normally addressed quickly were taking much longer to address. One day her personal computer seemed to have developed a virus, and she sent it off to be diagnosed and restored by their technical team. Three weeks passed, and her computer had not been returned, nor was she offered a loaner so she could continue her work.

She was told by a part-time contractor that they had a new computer for her, but it was being used for an event and they didn't know when she would receive it.

I can't imagine how someone can function effectively in a present-day workplace, let alone as a Program Director at a leading university, without access to email and the organization's system applications. This executive didn't realize that the person she would later approach to inquire about the status of her computer and the inefficient process was in The Club. Their discussion ended badly. The Club member turned the tables and brought other members into the fray, ultimately resulting in a complaint against the Program Director, even though the fact remained that she still did not have a computer and could not do her work. It should also be noted that the Club member was a woman, and she was supported in this matter by the top management.

I don't know what it is about computer equipment, but I had a similar experience when I was working for a financial services company as the national director for all operational-center Local Area Networks (LANs). I had a tight deadline to install LANs in three of six locations, and needed to test some new domain controllers before placing a larger order. I went through the normal procurement channels to obtain the domain controller equipment, and then I waited for the equipment to arrive. Typically, domain controllers would arrive within several weeks of placing an order, since they were a commodity-type of equipment. After about a month, I contacted the IT procurement director, who was my peer, and was informed by his assistant that someone else's order for the same equipment was treated as a priority, and mine would be processed later.

I responded like any other executive would have responded, which was to say that this was a 'dumb' process. I know that it wasn't the most elegant response, but it was an accurate assessment of the circumstances. In the end, The Club insured that their own members were taken care of, and I was reprimanded by my peer for being critical about the process. I had to wait several more weeks before my order was processed and before my LAN team could continue their work. In cases like these, The Club members will insure that they are not found to be complicit or at fault in throwing up roadblocks.

"User Error"

Resistance can come in many forms. The 'user error' technique is a common form of resistance that a Club relies on rather than trying to solve a problem presented by someone outside the Club. During my years at an engineering company, the senior management team was comprised of five men and one woman who led the marketing and sales division. The company was essentially a start-up business within a large multinational firm.

It was common for the company's senior executives to demonstrate the technology we were selling in real time to prospective clients. The engineering teams were always notified when the management team was making sales calls, since we were rolling out the technology in waves according to the size of the metropolitan area and specific location of large customers. The marketing executive usually knew in advance of her sales calls whether she would have access to the technology in order to conduct a successful demonstration. On one particular call with a potentially large customer, she called to say that the device and service were not working properly, and she asked for the engineering group to check out the issue immediately.

Some of the engineers performed a preliminary test, and it seemed that the service was working on our end. They didn't have the same sense of urgency as this executive, and their position was, "she shouldn't give demonstrations if she doesn't know how to use the device." It was a user error in their minds, and her position and role in the company held no special importance for them. The problem turned out to be a technical one. Because of the resistance from the engineers to treat the problem as they would from one of their own senior managers, it was much harder for the female executive to recover from the technical failure in front of a potential new client.

$- \square -$

Some resistance or conflict is expected

between people and organizations...

$- \square -$

"Lock Out"

In this same company, one of the most remarkable occurrences of resistance came when the senior vice president of engineering decided to lock down the office suite where the engineering group worked, to stop what he perceived to be myriad interruptions from the sales, marketing and implementation teams which were run by the same female executive mentioned above. He considered the interruptions disruptive to the software engineers' development and QA testing efforts. These engineers were responsible for product releases as well software modifications needed for the customers' applications to work properly over the network. The lock-down occurred during off hours, and when the sales/marketing and implementation teams returned to the office the next day, they were shocked to find that their entry cards for accessing the engineering group didn't work. In hindsight, it was quite funny to watch the teams' disbelief evolve into violent and desperate knocking on the engineers' doors. It was as if their favorite restaurant or theater closed down right in front of their eyes.

Some resistance or conflict is expected between people and organizations with diverging objectives and incentives. When it continues unchecked and/or veers into obstructionist behavior, it harms both the organization's bottom line and your ability to work effectively.

What you can do:

In the engineering company described above, the new CEO stepped in immediately. He not only had the engineering group's doors re-opened, he saw the resistance as an opportunity to develop stronger teamwork across the business silos and take down the walls of The Club. What may have on the surface been targeted bad behavior toward the head of sales and marketing turned out to be a broader team development issue across the company at all levels.

Seeking Support

Awareness that resistance is in play and understanding the root cause is key in dealing with resistance. First, seek out leaders with influence and someone you trust to help you interpret the root cause of the resistance, and enlist their help. I have found this to be one of the best ways to remove the roadblocks and foster communications. A strong branch needs a strong tree to support it. If your department's or division's charter clearly conflicts with the company's goals, or your directive is inflicting massive change in the business and you don't have the requisite chief executive-level or board support, then you need to raise awareness and enlist the support, or move on to avoid failure. Neither you nor your company will be successful in a 'no-win' environment.

"Likability" as a manager takes on greater weight for women executives than for men, and you will have to determine whether the resistance is simply tied to the likability factor — which isn't easy to rectify alone. In one experience I had in my career (thankfully there weren't many), the vice president of infrastructure and I were meeting regularly to discuss application testing plans for the disaster recovery solution our company was exploring. I took the meetings seriously and always wanted to insure we had the most current status on the plans for the application portfolio I was managing. After one of the regular meetings, I received a phone call from the VP asking me if he had done anything to offend me, since I seemed so serious and "unfriendly" toward him. Of course I assured him he had done nothing to offend me, but I became much more aware of the need to converse with him on a regular basis and build rapport.

He was very likeable, which made the resulting conversations easygoing and nonthreatening. Asking someone if you've offended them, or on the flip side, if there is something more you can do to align with their expectations, appears to be an effective way to clarify behaviors which can pave the way for rapport. I've kept that technique in my toolkit and use it when it's needed. However, it may not work in every instance of resistance. Enlisting the help of an intermediary such as a facilitator, an HR specialist or a coach works best when resistance is based on resentment, a perceived slight, or some other interpersonal issue. Although an intermediary may not rectify the problem permanently, I have facilitated many meetings between disparate parties over the years, and despite the fact we may have reached equilibrium at some point during the meeting, the resisting behavior often continued afterwards.

Double Standards

As a manager moving up the corporate ladder during the '80s and early '90s, I had little to draw upon with regard to how women should be in the workplace. If you look at the corporate attire of those days, most women wore suits and even ties to establish a level of professionalism and authority and, on some level, to emulate the men with whom they worked. Women had been advised over the years to be more like men in their thinking and behavior to be successful.

I don't buy into the idea that women should just be more like men, particularly because of the social context that drives normative female behaviors. Whether you buy into that theory for success or not, behavior that is accepted as "men being men" in the workplace is not accepted from a woman. All men and women executives should follow good management practices and business ethics, and espouse sound judgment to be successful, but a woman cannot slam her fist on the table or use forceful or unsavory language in a meeting room, or with a peer, without immediate backlash.

Although aggressive behavior from men is accepted as a sign of strength from both men and women, when the same type of behavior comes from a woman, it's perceived as irrational or even out of control. Aggression doesn't belong in the workplace—period. It doesn't matter which gender is displaying it. I believe that self-confidence is mistakenly aligned with aggressiveness rather than assertiveness, and many companies look past the destructive aspects that ensue because of it. The challenge that women executives face today is that they have worked alongside their male peers and have attempted to emulate the traits they believe represent strength and confidence, as well as likability. The vast majority of women I have worked with in my career were completely rational and level-headed. Even so, there are exceptions that unfortunately people remember, and these exceptions contribute to the idea that women can't be strong business leaders without crossing the aggression line.

— □ —

...women executives...have
attempted to emulate the traits they
believe represent strength...

— □ —

I hired a woman executive who was later promoted when I moved on in the organization. She wasn't combative or argumentative when she worked for me. Over time however, she became known for her combative interactions and was labeled 'the screamer' by her staff because her meetings often ended with her screaming about some issue. That's certainly one way to be heard by your staff, but for a woman, it plays out as another example of irrationality rather than strength, and it eventually calls one's competency as a leader into question.

A male executive admitted to me that he believes there are "absolutely double standards for women." He explained that the job descriptions and objectives are the same for men and women "on paper," but women "hold the burden of an undocumented set of standards" in terms of how they are expected to conduct themselves. The standard of behavior in his view is much higher for women.

Relationship Building

Another area where standards are significantly different between men and women—and an area that I approach here gingerly—deals with relationship building and loyalty to one's boss and superiors. Men influence their bosses and colleagues by developing a rapport with them, and they are more aggressive in building that rapport with their boss. This was the clearly the problem for the woman engineer I mentioned in Chapter 2 who was being excluded from lunches with her peers and who didn't have equal access to her boss. Women have to proceed more cautiously in developing a rapport with the boss, and in engaging a male mentor (particularly when there is no formal mentorship program in the company).

The sensitive part about this is how a woman is perceived when she cultivates a strong and loyal business relationship with her boss. If the organization is not Club-based, and the senior leaders of the organization are hiring and promoting women, such a relationship is not perceived negatively. Soon after I completed my MBA at Chicago Booth in the '90s, I got the entrepreneurial bug and launched a management consulting firm focused on IT strategy and business process reengineering. That experience was invaluable to me over the years because it gave me tremendous insight into different industries, organizational structures, and executive behaviors.

During a consulting engagement for an airline travel services company, I had the chance to work closely with the Chairman and CEO of a global internet travel reservation company. The Chairman had women executives reporting to him, and he was very open about discussing their career aspirations with them. He invited them to lunch, talked to them at company functions, and encouraged them. He also had a daughter that he mentored through college, and eventually through her career. On occasion, he would arrange for me to talk to his daughter about career opportunities when she was starting out. I realized that not all leaders have the panache that this executive had in working with women. A great deal relies on personality type, confidence and respect for individuals. This Chairman set the example for all others to follow and created a culture that fostered relationships across the gender divide without negative connotations attached to them.

Another CEO I had the fortune to meet through my husband had an illustrious career running one of the largest credit card companies in the U.S. before becoming the CEO of an internet financial services company. He was very comfortable working with women, and had several women on his senior executive team. He was also known for saying "I don't allow any ass—s to work for me." You can't send a clearer message than that to your management team with regard to how you want the team to operate!

It's difficult enough for a woman to build a relationship with a male boss and male peers in any organization. In a Club-based organization, unfortunately, such relationships can be viewed as something other than professional. There's often speculation that there is something more to the relationship if a woman is moving up the ranks. Of course this scenario can happen in any organization, but Club-based organizations don't acknowledge women's contributions or value them in the way they value their own members, so the fundamental beliefs of these organizations have the potential to demean women's credentials and foster a negative perception of women in general.

What you can do:

First and foremost, women have to be unflappable regardless of whether they are working in a Club-based organization or one that is more inclusive of their contributions. A woman's strengths must be channeled through directness and conciseness rather than brawn. All of the successful women executives I have interviewed singled out bad behavior from women as the most detrimental to their ability to achieve the company's goals. Although screaming and cursing from a male executive could be perceived as strength, these behaviors in women almost invariably incite negative labeling and diminished perceptions of women's competence. Double standards have to be addressed within your organization in the same way biases do.

What worked for me was to ask the person who was speculating about my business relationship with my boss, or a promotion, or a current assignment, "How is this different from my peers who have a good relationship with my boss or who were recently promoted?" A woman executive I interviewed who leads global marketing for a top network services provider described how she used humor to point out the suspicions her promotion raised with a male colleague who speculated she got the promotion because she was "good-looking." Her male colleague would have readily accepted a male peer's promotion over her promotion, and the woman executive recognized that she had the responsibility to address it. Her response was "You think I'm good-looking? Thank you for the compliment." She not only raised the awareness of the behavior, but gained a life-long supporter in the end.

CHAPTER 3:

Summary Points

☐ Be aware of the Six Lethal Barriers to The Club that can stifle your career goals and success, and be prepared to make decisions and take actions that will benefit you and your organization.

☐ Bullying and aggressiveness are not the same as passion and assertiveness and shouldn't be treated as such.

☐ Deep-rooted biases in both genders result in more hoops and hurdles for women to pass through and de-value women's accomplishments and contributions. Awareness of deep-rooted bias is the first step in addressing it.

☐ Don't sit in the audience. Provide clarity to your role.

☐ Budget disparity forces women to work longer and harder than their male counterparts and increases their risk of failure. Rely on data to set expectations about what can be realistically produced with your budget.

☐ Resistance can look and feel like a series of hurdles to be jumped over in a competitive race, and is expected to some degree in organizations with diverging objectives and incentives. When resistance veers into obstructionist behavior, it harms both your ability to work effectively and the organization's bottom line, and requires top-down support to correct it.

☐ A woman's strengths and relationships are viewed through a double-standard lens. What is accepted as "men being men" in the workplace is not accepted from a woman.

CHAPTER 4:

It Starts at the Top—
Acceptance of Club Culture in an Organization

THERE ARE TWO SCHOOLS OF THOUGHT regarding the role that corporate culture plays in deriving value for a corporation. One view diminishes the value of corporate culture and encourages a stringent focus on financial results and rewards for sales and profits, while the other view values the corporate culture as a competitive advantage. In the first view, labor is typically treated as a commodity, allowing frequent labor changes within the business to accommodate the business skills needed at a particular moment. Turnover is not considered a detriment. You see this approach in most consulting companies that focus on acquiring skill sets to support the latest trends in technology.

The second approach, in contrast, views labor as valuable assets and treats those assets as "talent" that requires nurturing, development, and incentives to stay within the organization.[23] Both types of corporate cultures foster Club behavior when the senior leadership teams, which are still predominately male, set the tone and maintain it. I interviewed women across a number of industries, and one striking example from academia illus-trates how the prevailing club behavior was excluding women from Department Chair and Dean-level positions.

Dr. Mary Lou Schmidt (Ch. 3) shared with me how she and a small group of women faculty members started their journey at the College of Medicine at the University of Illinois in 2002. An Association of American Medical Colleges (AAMC) confer-ence that year included data revealing an alarming lack of women in leadership positions at the 126 medical schools in the U.S., although women had been entering medical school in droves since the 1970s. Dr. Schmidt and the other women real-ized that external factors had to be a fundamental contributor to the scant representation of women in leadership positions at medical schools. At her own College of Medicine, 22 of the 23 Department Chairs were male, and thus women held only 4% of the leadership roles even though 50% of the College's medical student population was female. She recognized that changing the status quo at the UIC College of Medicine would be quite a challenge. She and five other women faculty mem-bers approached the Dean of UIC's College of Medicine in

2003 and asked for a meeting. Although the Dean was aware of the gender disparity among faculty members at all U.S. medical schools, he contended that the lack of women in leadership positions was a result of the talent pipeline, theorizing that women hadn't been in the pipeline long enough.

Dr. Schmidt's group requested and the Dean allowed the formation of a Faculty Academic Advancement Committee (FAAC) to develop and sponsor awareness-training sessions on unspoken biases. The group realized that gender bias awareness and support from the Dean would be critical success factors in influencing the department chairs, to change their views of women as leaders.

In introducing this new Dean's-level committee, Mary Lou was allowed only two minutes to speak at the Department Chairs' staff meeting to present the findings from the AAMC conference to the 23 assembled department chairs. Ultimately, multiple educational sessions on gender bias, the slow academic advancement of women, strategies for better recruitment of women candidates and individual data on faculty advancement, retention and recruitment were brought to the department chairs and the 800 faculty members at UIC. Eventually, all of the UIC departments' statistics regarding gender and underrepresented minorities in comparison with national data were required in the department chairs' annual reviews.

Although the Dean did not create the FAAC committee or aggressively promote the activities of this committee, his approval of the launch of the FAAC in 2003 was viewed as the first positive step toward addressing gender disparity. Progress has been slow but encouraging. As of January 2012, 17% of the department chair positions at the UIC College of Medicine were held by women (4 of 23 positions vs. 1 of 23 in 2003). This would not have occurred without a small group of motivated women starting at the top and establishing a diverse committee that was willing to be patient, willing to share and discuss the data openly, and willing to work through the resistance that comes with change.

The Type of Industry Doesn't Matter

In my career, the leaders who stood out among their peers with regard to setting the cultural tone and leading by example came from different industries: wireless data products, banking, and credit card services, shattering the notion that certain industries are more apt to hire and promote women. In my resistance example from Chapter 3, I mentioned how quickly the CEO of the engineering company recognized the negative impact of the resisting behaviors by his engineering team when they locked down their office suite to prevent interruptions from the marketing and sales organization, and how effectively the CEO addressed them. He used that incident as a springboard to cultivate both his leadership vision and the internalized beliefs and outward behaviors he expected to see from his management team. From that point forward, every person in the company attended team-building training, and new processes and techniques were developed to increase cross-functional participation in all business functions. This was an environment where I personally felt I could contribute to the best of my abilities and where I and many of my peers flourished, because of the cultural and behavioral framework that was put into place from the top to guide the organization toward its goals.

So why do some companies get it right and reap the benefits of an inclusive organization for their shareholders and employees, and others don't? It takes a certain type of leader to create and lead an organization that recognizes and capitalizes on the talents of women. The companies that 'statistically' get it right and lead the pack in representing women on their boards and executive teams, such as Xerox, Marriott, and IBM, as well as those that culturally get it right like IBM, have proven through their bottom lines and rankings as Fortune 500 companies that they are benefiting from their decision to prevent or break the Club culture and include women on their leadership teams.

− □ −

...some leaders still believe that they are setting the bar high and women just can't reach the standard.

− □ −

The companies and organizations that don't get it must be holding on to outdated organizational hierarchies and behaviors. It may also be that some leaders still believe that they are setting the bar high and women just can't reach the standard. Is it coincidental that Xerox's board is 30% women when its CEO, Ursula Burns, is leading the company, or that PepsiCo's senior management team is 27% women when Indra Nooyi is the CEO? It takes women leading women and men leading organizations that nurture women's talents and capitalize on their contributions to allow women to succeed. It also takes awareness of the biases that prevent women from getting in the door in the first place.

Men and women shared their experiences with me about the importance of fitting in with the culture of the organization. In the Club-based organizations, I learned from these executives that fitting in with the culture took precedence over every other facet of a woman's resume.

So how does a leader break through the standard ways of attracting and keeping talent regardless of gender? The Founder and Chairman of an innovative credit card payment and services company discovered that the one of the most important critical success factors for growing his business was to develop a culture of "builders and creators". Initially it was a struggle to find resources with the technical, business process acumen and customer service experience the company needed, so they did the unthinkable—they hired 55 people based on a set of qualities, not just on industry or technical experience, and they trained and coached them. They looked for people who were educated, self-starters, customer-focused, and team players. Each employee receives direct feedback from peers and customers and is encouraged to voice their ideas and opinions in regularly scheduled town hall meetings. The company quickly realized that they didn't need managers because they hired smart and talented people who upheld the cultural values of their company, including mutual respect for their peers regardless of gender.

I'm not proposing that software companies should stop hiring engineers, or law firms should stop hiring lawyers, but the example of this entrepreneurial company suggests that the executive teams in most companies could be looking at talent in the wrong ways. My career path actually followed a similar pattern. I was hired by an innovative health insurance company that wanted to bring in talented individuals from diverse backgrounds and train them on their technology and business processes in order to design a new and innovative insurance system. It turned out to ignite my passion for IT as well as provide firm-specific knowledge with the company's automated claim payment system that was not easily acquired from other places.

– □ –

...understand the cultural tone from the top before you step into the position...

– □ –

As a woman starting a career or a woman looking for the next step in a career, it's important to understand the cultural tone from the top before you step into the position and the company. The following chapters will help raise awareness regarding what data and behaviors to look for, and what environmental elements are needed for women to thrive in leadership positions. You may still decide to work in a Club-based organization, but at least you can do so with an understanding of what lies ahead, and you'll be armed with techniques that will allow you to perform and advance within that culture.

CHAPTER 4:

Summary Points

☐ The senior leadership team sets the cultural tone in every organization.

☐ Many senior managers and C-level leaders are not aware of the scant representation of women leaders in their organizations, and don't necessarily believe that a diverse organization will benefit their employees or their company's bottom line.

☐ It takes women leading women and men leading organizations that nurture women's talents and capitalize on their contributions to allow women to succeed.

☐ Companies would benefit more from hiring "builders and creators" rather than from narrowly defined experiences that promote bias.

☐ It's important to understand the cultural tone from the top before you step into a new position or company.

CHAPTER 5:

Getting to the Core of Club Behavior —

How to Spot It *Before* You're Hired

It's one thing to see Club members bullying non-members within your own organization, but how do you ferret out that behavior, as well as the other Club traits, before you accept an executive-level position, or any position at a new company? There are several metrics that need to be pursued assertively with the potential boss and peers at the new company. Taken as a whole, the answers to these metrics will provide a great deal of insight into the general culture of the company, and they'll highlight the degree of Club-based behavior and the degree of support you can expect as a woman executive.

– □ –

As long as companies remain profitable, boards of directors won't encourage diversity...

– □ –

What percent of the senior management team and board are women?

I have found this question to be unnerving when presented to most interviewers, including women. The recruiters, HR executives and senior management teams should know these statistics the same way they know their profit and loss numbers, or how much cash flow the company is generating. From my experience though, most companies do not track how many women or minorities they have within their management ranks. The reasons are that (a) their numbers are not flattering let alone encouraging, and (b) they don't feel that there is a compelling reason to measure these numbers. As long as companies remain profitable, boards of directors won't encourage diversity—unless the board members are well acquainted with companies that provide better performance as a result of a diverse management team, and/or someone on the board is an advocate of a balanced team.

Although women represent over 50% of the U.S. workforce and are now receiving more advanced degrees than men, they are grossly underrepresented in management ranks across industries. As of 2009, roughly 13% of corporate officer-level positions were held by women.[24] Within the span of my 30-year career, I've heard and read numerous explanations about the gap between women's presence in the workforce and their representation in senior management (as if explaining the gap justified it). The most common explanation is that women leave work to raise their children. The work hours lost during child rearing alone don't account for a 37% loss of representation in the management ranks. Of course there are the explanations that "women aren't studying the right things," or that "men are better suited for executive positions." But these claims are unsupported.

Fortunately, it is relatively easy to extract the answer yourself by perusing the company's website and noting the makeup of the most-senior leadership team. What's more difficult to see of course is the makeup of the less-senior vice presidents who are not listed on those websites, which can give you insight into how well the company is stocking the pipeline. The revelation is in the details. Fewer women in the downstream executive positions result in fewer women fueling the most senior leadership track. So, it's important to extract those details. Don't be alarmed if the recruiter, human resource director, or your prospective boss doesn't have the data.

If the metric is available, there is a high probability that the percentage of senior management-level women and officers in the company is 25% or lower.[25] If you review the Fortune 500 companies from 2011 as I did below in Chart 1,[26] you'll find that women's representation ranges from a flat zero on the low end to 25% on the high end. For board positions, the average remains at approximately 15% across all companies.[27] What's remarkable about this sample is that half of the Top 10-ranked Fortune 500 companies have no women on their senior management teams. No women in senior management means no pipeline to CEO positions, which also means fewer opportunities for board service, since the majority of current boards want members with at least six years of board experience.[28]

Chart 1

F 500 Rank	2011 Fortune 500 Company	Top 5 Execs Women/Men	Percent	Board Members Women/Men	Percent
1	Walmart	0/5	0	1/15	6%
2	Exxon Mobil	0/5	0	1/11	8%
3	Chevron	1/4	20%	0/11	0%
4	ConocoPhillips	1/4	20%	3/9	25%
5	Fannie Mae	1/4	20%	1/10	9%
6	General Electric	1/4	20%	4/12	25%
7	Berkshire Hathaway	0/2	0	2/12	14%
8	General Motors	0/5	0	2/7	22%
9	Bank of America	1/4	20%	2/11	15%
10	Ford Motor	0/5	0	2/17	11%
18	IBM	3/17	15%	2/10	17%
30	Home Depot (top 8 execs)	1/7	13%	2/8	20%
35	Apple	0/5	0	1/6	14%
42	Wellpoint (top 8 execs)	2/8	20%	5/8	38%
83	News Corp.	1/5	17%	1/16	6%
95	Time Warner (top 6 execs)	1/5	17%	2/11	15%
121	Xerox	1/5	20%	3/7	30%

For example, 17% (one out of six) of News Corporation's executive officers as of their June 2011 Annual Report were women. This is well above the 13% average for women in corporate officer positions as reported by Catalyst. Delving further into several of News Corporation's business units, you would find the key executives for Twentieth Century Fox Film Corporation to be 20% women (one of five), one of the highest in the sample, while the percentage of female key executives in Fox Cable Networks Inc. and Fox Broadcasting Company Inc. is 0%.[29]

Apple Inc., on the other hand, has no women on its senior executive team, and only one woman on their board. I have made several visits to Apple stores in Los Angeles and Chicago since 2008, and I repeatedly noticed that male "genius"-level sales staff (Apple's term) far out-numbered the females on the sales floor. However, on my most recent trips (in 2011), I noticed more women staffers in the stores. If the ratio of women to men genius-level staffers remains low, fewer women will have the product and service experience needed to move up the management ranks. Obviously, Apple is a wildly successful company. The stock trades at triple-digit numbers, and people buy millions of Apple products each year.

However, the point of presenting the percentage of women on Apple's senior management team is for you to determine whether women who are interested in the opportunity to work at Apple and have aspirations to ascend the management ladder would be accepted and successful in the company.

The labor statistics confirm that there are few women in senior leadership positions in *any* corporation, although there are notable exceptions to the dismal data in the table above, such as Wellpoint and Xerox. But why ask the question about women's representation on executive teams and boards if we can predict the answer? The importance of the question lies in whether or not the company is keeping pace with the labor market and taking strides to make cultural changes. Asking why there are so few women at senior levels and what the company is doing to attract or promote women is really the key here.

− □ −

...diversity programs and affinity groups...were grossly ineffective.

− □ −

Even so, I've worked in companies with diversity programs and affinity groups and found that such efforts were grossly ineffective in changing the behavior of the company with respect to hiring, promoting and retaining women in executive-level positions. Unless these programs address the biases and underlying beliefs that create exclusive behavior in Club-based management teams, women will continue to be underrepresented in senior level roles in the workplace.

If you are starting out in your management career, be particularly attentive to the percentage of women in the pipeline and the percentage that transition to management positions. Bad numbers are bad numbers no matter what the company spokesperson says. As noted above, at Walmart, 86% of the 3,400 managers are men, even though women represent 66% of their workforce. They also have zero women on their senior management team, and are far below the 15% average representation of women on their board.

What's the tenure of the senior management team?

The answer to this question should be evaluated in conjunction with the question on overall turnover rate. If the average tenure of the senior executive team is over 15 years, it would be best to know whether this long tenure is because (a) the company is a great place to work, (b) the executive team has consistently outperformed their industry peers, or (c) a Club is firmly imbedded in the organization. If the turnover rate for non-executive positions is high while tenure at the executive suite is high, it likely corroborates the existence of a strong, exclusive management Club leading to a drain of talent across the company.

There are exceptions, of course. For example, in January 2011, Google gave all of its employees a raise to stave off defections to its rival, Facebook. The reasons given by many for the exodus from Google had more to do with incentives such as higher pay, plus renewed excitement for working for a company that was rumored to be going public, rather than leaving a Club-based management team.

How is succession planned?

When you're assessing a company to determine whether it has a Club culture, another issue to consider is the manner in which employees move up the ladder to senior-level positions and spots on the board of directors. Another way to look at succession is to explore how much is spent in dollars and time on executive development across the company (and in particular for the business unit or division you may be entering or leading). As executives, we all want to keep the best-trained personnel in our divisions and companies. Companies often determine who is eligible for participation in executive-level education and development, and it's important to know up front how you can tap into that.

At a Motorola subsidiary I worked for in the early to mid-90s, the management team was asked to participate in a Meyers-Briggs[30] leadership assessment periodically throughout their tenure. These were self-assessments, and there was a significant amount of time dedicated to training the management team on the use of this tool. A leadership coach reviewed the results with each manager so that we understood the significance of our specific leadership profile. We then shared our respective profiles with the other managers. While the assessments gave us good insight into our own profiles such as how we preferred to work (e.g., up front and center vs. behind the scenes) or how we preferred to acquire and absorb information (details vs. main points), the real benefit came from understanding our peers' and bosses' preferences compared to our own results. It improved our ability to recognize different styles and traits and make adjustments in our styles to become more effective executives. In terms of relationship building, it steered us away from making false assumptions about a person because he or she didn't see things the same way, which is a fundamental contributor to "Group Think" and bias.

I recently worked with an organization that conducts assessments for executives who have a desire to serve on boards of directors. After a self-assessment, the company compares the executive's skills and experience to those of current boards in their database and allows the individual to make informed career choices to reach his or her goals.

There are many types of formal programs that companies offer to executives who aspire to be in the pool of candidates for senior-level positions, whether through leadership assessments, rotating assignments or leadership development programs that will enable you to be considered in a succession plan. To be considered in a company's succession plan, you need to be aware of the process for bringing executives into the pipeline, and you'll need to articulate your interest upfront, during the hiring process.

What is the turnover rate?

In a mature company, voluntary turnover remains a primary metric for how well the company is retaining its top talent. It could also indicate how well a company recruits its top talent and how effective the recruiters are at determining a cultural fit. If the overall turnover at a company is high and there are no known external factors affecting the exodus (such as incentives to join another firm, potential merger and acquisition activity, or outsourcing initiatives), further evaluation and a deeper understanding of the root cause of the turnover are necessary. Some industries—such as technology outsourcing firms— expect turnover within their ranks to be around 11%. Competition for technology-savvy employees across these firms is high, and companies will commonly entice such employees to leave their current company for a better opportunity.

When linked to the question on tenure and percentage of women on the senior management team, the turnover rate reflects the effectiveness of the senior management team in creating a culture and a company where people want to work. When interviewing, don't settle for "I've been here for 20 years" from the person conducting the interview as representative of the culture. Press for the metrics if you want to see the warning signs up front.

Which undergraduate and graduate schools are the executives pulled from?

This question probes the potential for exclusivity and lack of diversity in the management ranks. If a limited number of schools or only the schools attended by the senior management team are tapped for executive candidates, you've got to consider how this will affect you. It's also not uncommon for recruiters and interviewers to have implicit preferences for certain schools and programs. Although I understand the rationale for supporting one's alma mater (whether undergraduate or graduate programs) and encouraging recruitment from one's school, these unstated biases can limit your success and career advancement in the company, especially if you are unaware of the biases.

The arguments for targeting recruiting from select institutions depend on a host of logical factors ranging from specialization in certain fields of study — such as finance, engineering, marketing or international and entrepreneurial studies — to locality. Synergies abound when companies are located near an institution providing a strong talent pool, which is why so many start-up companies are located in Silicon Valley near Stanford, and technology companies are near the Research Triangle in North Carolina. What you will be looking for is a pattern of candidate selection that is (or is not) warranted based on the business model.

What are the formal opportunities for management team-building?

Management team-building is another issue to be aware of when you're considering a company. Having lunch with every one of your peers individually is a positive thing, but if your boss or your peers expect you to build team relationships on your own as a Club outsider, you won't make much progress. This holds true for men and women. I've seen this happen consistently with executives across industries as well as from my own experiences.

I worked with a male senior account executive from a leading consulting firm for over a year. As one of his major clients, he spent a great deal of time meeting with me and my peers over lunch, dinner, or cocktails. He even met with my staff periodically and held parties for them when project milestones were met. His own firm expected him to spend time with our company's leadership team, many of whom were Club members, and funded his entertainment budget appropriately. After great effort on his part, the rewards didn't materialize. He was spread too thin, and he was challenged by the Club's lack of cooperation for a project that was formally sponsored by the Club's very own CEO and CFO. His relationships with the Club members within our company eventually deteriorated, and he left the engagement.

How did this happen? There was no formal mechanism to build working relationships between his firm and the client executives. He assumed, like the average person would, that the importance of the high-profile project alone would be sufficient to develop a team. But as we've seen, being outside the Club means you will have little or no influence on how the Club members choose to operate.

Companies that value functional and diverse management teams regularly plan and hold management sessions, or what is typically known as 'off-site' meetings with the management teams. These meetings include a wide variety of topics and are valuable in training a management team on how to engage each other to the benefit of the company and its shareholders. These types of sessions become even more important when companies are experiencing major change within their business or organizational structure because they can focus on the big picture and the expected behavior.

Many companies I've worked for provided executives with opportunities to attend executive-level education courses, as well as advanced degree programs from top universities, covering a broad range of business and technical disciplines. It's important to know at the onset what the criteria are for participating in these programs and how to avail yourself of the opportunities.

What are the opportunities for career growth?

Just about every company I've worked for had a career "ladder." You start as a manager overseeing a certain number of people and budget, and then move up after enough knowledge is accumulated to a senior manager, director, vice president, etc. The real reason behind this question is to understand the formal and informal practices the company has for rewarding hard work and providing new opportunities.

Some of these practices include the use of formal mentors, such as the IBM mentoring program described by the female executive in Chapter 3, or job rotation such as the one The Walt Disney Company executed in 2009 by swapping the roles of two of their top executives: Jay Rasulo, who was the Parks and Resorts Chairman at that time, became the Chief Financial Officer, while Tom Staggs, who held the Chief Financial Officer position, stepped into the Parks and Resorts role.

It's helpful to speak to people within the organization you are interested in about their growth opportunities and what made it happen for them. Proceed with caution if the response to this question is vague, or is described as limitless providing you work hard. I've heard from many women who were given serial opportunities very much in line with their current skill set that didn't "stretch" them enough to break through the Club barriers and allow them to move up in the organization.

I was fortunate to work for many companies that introduced me to new functions and allowed me to create new things. For example, at a time when I was asked to start an Office of the CIO for a large Fortune 500 company, I was over-seeing global application development and support for the company. In that role, I was solely focused on service delivery for over 20 business entities. The new opportunity gave me a chance to see how the IT division operated from another viewpoint in terms of which technologies and vendors we should engage and what methodologies we should employ universally to deliver quality results. That experience led to knowledge acquisition around managing risk, and a subsequent IT Governance Officer role.

It's good to understand how these opportunities develop within the organization. In some cases you may be stepping into a role and a large corporate culture where you will be the lone scout leading the charge, as it was for me. If that suits you, then the company may be a good fit for you. Taken in conjunction with the answers on the tenure of the senior management team and how succession plans are accomplished, you will get a sense of how static the company's organizational structure is and whether you will have the opportunity to achieve your career goals as a woman in your target company.

How is performance evaluated?

If performance is evaluated on how likeable you are, then run for the door. You're doomed from the start if the key traits the company desires are described as "collaborative," "relationship builder," "service-oriented," or "team player," when no objective data or assessment system is in place to determine whether you hit those marks. If you are stepping into a leadership role, don't settle for a description of the evaluation process that *you* will give your direct reports. Delve into what criteria you can expect to see from your boss. What are those top five goals and metrics he or she expects you to hit, and how are the data compiled? Without knowing the answer, you may end up with continually shifting priorities that don't jive with the overall strategy of the company.

—□—

Club members will continue to rely on heuristics and likability traits to determine performance.

—□—

This is critical for executive women, since the restricted information flow and networking opportunities limit their ability to meet or exceed the companies' expectations. Pay for performance is gaining popularity, but the objective measurement systems have not kept pace with the concept. Therefore companies, and particularly Club members, will continue to rely on heuristics and likability traits to determine performance and pay.

CHAPTER 5:

Summary Points

Questions to Ask a Potential Employer

☐ What percent of the senior management team and Board is comprised of women?

☐ What's the tenure of the senior management team?

☐ What is the turnover rate?

☐ How is succession planned?

☐ Which undergraduate and graduate schools are the executives pulled from?

☐ What are the formal opportunities for management team-building?

☐ What are the opportunities for growth?

☐ How is performance evaluated?

Tips from the Front Lines —
Critical Elements of Success

THE FOLLOWING CRITICAL ELEMENTS OF SUCCESS are the core principles I used to build my IT skills at every stage of my career, whether as a Network Manager, LAN Manager, Head of Enterprise Architecture, Chief Technology Officer, Head of Worldwide Application Services, or IT Governance Officer. They also reflect the attitudes and tips from many of the successful women I've known, as well wisdom from my mentors over the years. It's really all about having choices and making choices in your current work environment and throughout your career. No one has full control over their work environment (or lives, for that matter), but these critical elements of success are under your control in the sense that you can put them into practice over time. Some of the elements take time to cultivate while others can be put into practice immediately by changing the way you approach your work and your relationship with your environment.

Do your best work every day regardless of the culture or political climate.

Another way of phrasing this critical element of success is to "stick to your guns" and perform in the best interest of the company, your staff, your customers and your shareholders every single day with diligence and quality. Gather your sources and data, and be prepared. Approach work as an evolution. You may move on in your career and find that you're re-assuming a function or a team that you established several years earlier, or find that you're living with your previous work and decisions down the road.

An example of this is when I led the enterprise architecture group for a large corporation. My first task was to establish a set of standard components for the various layers in the technology stack. I enlisted the help of an IT consulting firm and began working with each of the technology owners to gather the data and understand the pros and cons of their preferences. We selected about 100 components — a good starting point — and because of the diligence and effort that were applied during the process, many of the selected components remained implemented as viable technologies 10 years later.

An added plus for me was when I was moving on in my career, a database analyst who was recruited to support the database selection for our enterprise resource planning system thanked me for making the selections we did because it gave him a lasting and successful career. Although the objective of painstakingly evaluating and selecting technology platforms wasn't to enhance specific careers, this example does illustrate the potential longer-term effects of the work you do every day and highlights the sphere of influence you may not have realized you possess.

$-\square-$

...*enable yourself to do your best work within the constraints.*

$-\square-$

Doing your best work every day isn't easy regardless of the industry or size of an organization. "Good work" is debatable, particularly when adequate objective measurements are lacking (as is the case in most corporate structures). In the absence of objective measurements, following the core management practices is the best route.

For example, economic principles have remained constant in the IT world for the 30 years that I've been working in the field. The economic view of IT work predicts that (a) there will always be competition for scarce resources, and (b) prioritization is fundamental to staying focused on the most important aspects of technology work. The demand for services may continue to grow at exponential rates, while resources and budget remain fixed. Our history in a free market-driven economy tells us that companies will experience massive change during market disruptions, intense competition, and economic downturns, which will force once-important items to idle for awhile, or even drop off the radar.

HP (Hewlett Packard), for example, halted production of their TouchPad device and then discounted the price to sell off their excess inventory, which in turn increased market demand for the devices. In the end, HP wanted to refashion the company as a software provider, which meant exiting the tablet market and shifting away from the associated WebOS software, ultimately ending the company's reign as a legacy hardware company. These types of events don't necessarily make customers, employees, or shareholders happy, even if the strategic shift is driven by the board of directors. Your cus-tomers — and particularly Club members within your company — will expect you to carry on exactly as you did before the economic or business changes, which is why your best efforts have to be directed toward the highest priorities. You have to enable yourself to do your best work within the constraints, and speak to those constraints clearly and unapologetically.

For the majority of my career, my efforts have been supported and rewarded even when the decisions, process and system changes, or organizational structures were not popular, because the due diligence and quality were there. A woman executive who led global marketing for a leading network service company (Ch. 3) stated, "Everybody wants things. The higher up you go, the more expectations you have placed on you." She went on to say that it becomes imperative to "take control — you don't have to respond to everything." Looking at work through a quality control lens, quality results require a stringent focus on getting the key elements of the process or product right. If you try to adjust everything all the time, you no longer have a predictable and consistent outcome.

One CIO whom I worked for was particularly skilled in maneuvering the ship during difficult times. Most companies have their catch phrases for defining a lean environment, and he would refer to the constraints and the shift to a more focused mindset as operating in a "lights on" mode. Even with that articulation he was often surprised at how difficult it was for his own senior team to lessen their desires for new systems and enhancements that weren't funded, solely because of the shift in company priorities. In my senior IT role at this company, the customers of our demand-tracking system were from finance as well as the IT organization. My team had just completed the first phase of the demand-tracking system by integrating it with our labor-tracking application, allowing us to build capital projects from the ground up in terms of labor hours, skill sets, and costs needed for that particular effort.

After that initial implementation, change requests were coming in at a rapid pace to add functionality. This is a standard phase of post-project deployment. You want new ideas and suggested improvements to come from the constituents who interact with the system. For example, the finance executives wanted to attach a data mart to the system so that they could develop their own reports, and the IT executives wanted to add job scheduling functionality. The interesting phenomenon was that these executives, who would never consider starting a systems project without adequate resources or funding, expected our current support team to slip their change requests in during the team's spare time.

There was no spare time, of course, and nothing is as easy as it appears on the surface. My team diligently collected all of the requests, prioritized them with their input, and then assessed the cost. Once those data were available, we presented them to the CIO for approval, and he began crossing out line after line of requests. We ended with a small enhancement budget to make only the changes that were the most important to the company. The finance and IT executives were a bit stunned, since this was a far cry from the $30 million-or-so projects they were used to seeing.

In the end, everyone was redirected to the overriding task at hand, which was to shift the internal IT service delivery model toward an external outsourcing model. My team subsequently made the changes to the system that were funded, and we made sure that those changes functioned as designed. We didn't satisfy everyone, but we did the best work under the constraints.

Diligence and quality make a difference, even in the face of political fury, or when decisions, changes, and outcomes aren't popular. For women, having support from the top for decisions and services that are not popular with the Club is particularly important because it redirects the focus to the expectations, constraints and solutions rather than a woman's ability to deliver.

Earlier in my career, while at a financial services company, I was managing a systems development team responsible for designing and implementing the first financial planning system for the company, called "the Plan on the LAN." By all measures, the implementation was a success. Financial planning could be accomplished simply and simultaneously across departments. We rolled the system out to the home office and established guidelines for support. The support structure was "5x12," meaning that it provided onsite support five days per week for 12 hours at a time, from 8:00 am to 8:00 pm.

Soon after the roll-out, a number of planners came in on the weekend and quickly realized that there was no one from IT in the building to address their questions. Even though my budget didn't include funding the additional weekend support staff, we quickly set up a communication mechanism so that weekend workers' could notify my LAN group when they would be working weekends, and I could adjust the coverage accordingly. Even with the constraints, the solution worked adequately enough to support the planning process. It was the best solution given the constraints.

Stay Calm, Carry On, and Remain Fierce

One of the most positive effects an executive woman can have on the Club culture is to remain unflappable at all times: staying calm, carrying on, and remaining fierce internally. On the surface this may sound trivial, but it is one of the most difficult things to master. I talked about double standards in Chapter 3 (Club Behaviors), and while it may sometimes be beneficial for male peers to lose their composure in the workplace, it is not beneficial for a woman executive in any way.

– □ –

...establish boundaries.

– □ –

The best way to develop composure is to practice. Anticipate what the counterpoints may be to your ideas. Think about how you will face complaints that are brought to you about your employees, your products, your service domains, or

119

even you. First, listen to complaints carefully and completely, and then establish boundaries for yourself so that you can approach the situation as a problem to solve rather than a personal issue. Remember, women often take on the role of fixing problems to everyone's satisfaction, which just isn't possible. Situations can and do get personal in a Club culture, and it's important to be prepared for the possibility that a situation will escalate beyond reasonable proportions.

One fruitful example I faced of staying calm and remaining fierce internally came during an onslaught of organizational and business changes from a cost-cutting initiative. I have always made a practice of hiring people with the best fit for their role (and hopefully for the organization), but not everyone turned out to be a good fit within the culture. I searched for months to fill a new vice president-level Total Cost of Ownership role and hired a woman who was credentialed, articulate, and a self- starter. She would be in a staff position which typically has a low acceptance rate in an IT group, where every resource is highly scrutinized for their perceived value. After a few short months of her arrival, I agreed to assign her to an IT outsourcing project with a focus on helping the senior management team analyze and design the functional roles that would be retained in each IT unit.

She was shunned by my peers right out of the gate, and subsequently I was faced with the daunting responsibility of listening to complaints about her from my peers and HR. Many of my peers descended on the HR manager to complain about her. Likability was definitely a factor raised by a few outspoken members of the Club. The key to sorting through the emotional issues was to uncover the fundamental driver for the "dislike." The culture of the organization was such that likability and relationships held a greater value than diligence and performance.

Foremost there was a communication style that had to be addressed. Both my peers and my boss were challenged by this employee's directness. Secondly, there was a trust issue, not just with my employee but across my entire peer group. During the organizational analysis phase, my peer group felt that each peer was stacking his or her retained organization with more positions than they needed. Some of them just wanted parity in organization size rather than focusing on what skill sets should be outsourced. They were taking their cues from the CIO, and he was wielding the ax so to speak, and I knew I couldn't change that.

There was a great deal of uncertainty in the situation. No one on the IT management team, or in the company for that matter, had in-depth experience with a large-scale outsourcing initiative that impacted hundreds of local jobs. There was tremendous fear that if the senior management team miscalculated anything, the business couldn't function.

In "Men and Women of the Corporation," originally published in 1977, Rosabeth Moss Kanter describes the behavior of corporations during high uncertainty in this way: "It is the uncertainty quotient in managerial work, as it has come to be defined in the large modern corporation, that causes management to become so socially restricting... to keep control in the hands of socially homogeneous peers."

I believe that the Club's rejection of a competent woman despite her contributions is a clear reflection of Ms. Kanter's observations, confirming that behaviors haven't changed much in over 30 years. With regard to the dilemma with her, after dozens of conversations that included HR, my boss, my peers and my employee, I was able to see that my employee's performance was clearly not the issue. In fact, she worked tirelessly in a role that she was not originally hired to perform. There were valid concerns to work on, though.

She and I stayed calm, carried on and remained fierce. She adjusted her communication style and approach, while I raised awareness of the difficult role thrust upon her. A year later, she became accepted and even appreciated for the service she provided, and I was supported by my boss and HR in giving her a performance appraisal and bonus that truly reflected her contribution.

A major factor in remaining fierce internally is not succumbing to the noise. In a Club-based organization, where everyone follows the cues of the Club and piles on their opinions accordingly, you can't lose sight of your management principles, core values, and beliefs.

Match your work ethic to the business strategy and expectations of your role.

Because of our innate tendencies to make every aspect of our work "right," women typically exert Herculean efforts to repair and nurture relationships, processes, organizations and systems throughout their careers. Although women perceive this as a strength and as a way to differentiate themselves from their competition and peers, it can be detrimental to their success as a leader when the organization, company, or their boss wasn't expecting them to make everything right—in other words, doing the work instead of delegating the work can and will be constraining.

In organizations where results can be objectively measured, it will be easier to focus on repairing and nurturing the areas that are impeding the results. However, most companies have subjective and ambiguous goals. For example, measuring increased sales revenue year over year sounds straightforward, but it is wrought with complexity. Have your sales revenue increased because of great sales strategies and market penetration, or is it because prices have increased while the number of units sold remains flat? Has customer satisfaction increased because you actually improved service levels, or is it because your boss no longer seems to be getting as many problem escalations or perhaps you only received a handful of responses to your customer satisfaction surveys and the data just happen to be skewed positively?

— □ —

...most companies have subjective and ambiguous goals.

— □ —

It's imperative to know whether the company is looking for innovation, lower operating costs, improved quality, or some other goal so that your efforts can be directed toward the work that ultimately achieves the company's goals, and primarily, so you don't overwork and spend time in areas that won't propel your career. Content may be "king" in the media and entertainment business, but strategy is everything in the business world and in IT. According to Joshua Ehrlich, founder of the Global Leadership Council, "many managers still spend too much time doing and not enough time thinking."[31]

While attending the 2011 Management Conference at the University of Chicago Booth School of Business, James E. Schrager, Clinical Professor of Entrepreneurship and Strategic Management, challenged the attendees to view the relationships between strategy, management, and pure luck within their own businesses in order to make better decisions in the future. He defined strategy as a clearly focused plan for the business, while management took on the necessary actions to implement the plan. Luck was just that, an occurrence or result that requires no plan or action. Luck just happens. Without knowing the plan or ideas about the business, the 'doing' part becomes speculative work.

IT organizations are typically positioned in one of two ways within a company, either as a strategic partner within the business units, or as a cost center focused on delivering service at the lowest price point. If you're in the latter category, it's best to understand that up front and look for ways to achieve that goal first, rather than expending all of your energy trying to change the ordained view of your organization and the expectations of your role.

I've seen many executives, both women and men, try to respond to every desire from the Club. This happens because in the absence of clear strategies from the most senior levels of the company, it's easy to fall into a "repair and nurture" cycle, reactively "fixing" every issue placed in front of them, and nurturing an outcome that takes valuable resources away from the outcomes that are critical to the company's future.

I was fortunate to learn the lesson of deciphering the top priorities from the 'noise' through a conscious selection process during my consulting years, from the Chairman and CEO of an electronic travel systems company that provided software services to airlines and travel agencies. I was working with several members of his management team evaluating internal sales processes and systems, and we were discussing alternatives for their current systems to achieve modest improvements in efficiency and reporting. He listened intently and then asked the head of marketing and sales to share the revenue streams coming from the international offices that would be impacted by the changes, and how these changes would improve the sales cycles.

After listening carefully, his assessment of investing capital in a legacy system without a fundamental business process change was "this system is broken, it can't be fixed." At that point, we all knew we had to look at other solutions that would provide more substantial change to the business at a faster rate, rather than expending more time on fixing and nurturing systems and processes that no longer met the needs of the company.

There are exceptions of course to avoiding the repair and nurture cycle. In some cases you are the designated change agent and you are expected to fix specific areas of your company. I've been in these types of roles at several points in my career and have found that linking your efforts back to the strategy is key, because without strategic alignment, everything becomes a priority and everyone needlessly contributes to your workload.

I worked for a large public company that did not have a documented IT strategy until I fostered and nurtured its development. You may run into the same situation; you would have to establish a prioritization process and push for your peers and senior team to articulate the connection between your responsibilities and the business goals. Without clearly articulated priorities, the special interests of the Club become the company's priorities, and the organization may be "broken" and "can't be fixed."

Take on new roles and assignments only when the work is supported up front.

I have always encouraged women to take on new responsibilities as a way to prepare them for the next step in their careers. Doing so worked in my favor, but I learned that discussions about the resources and capital necessary to assume the added responsibility must take place before you leap at the new opportunity. It's much more difficult to say "I can't be successful without certain skills or assets" at a later date. No one would expect a President to function without a Chief of Staff, or a system developer to test code in a production environment.

It's reasonable to ask for basic infrastructure needs, and yet women are not comfortable doing it. I interviewed a young woman who was starting her management career at a recruitment firm in the Chicago area. She was excited to be promoted to a Manager, and readily accepted the position. What they didn't tell her up front was that she was expected to continue to handle her current workload in addition to overseeing a small staff. She quickly discovered that her salary did not change, and her work environment did not change. She remained in her cubicle alongside her peers, making it impossible for her to have meetings or one-on-one sessions. She did what most women would do in her situation, and that was to work longer hours. When the hives she developed from the stress became unbearable, she did what most women would do, which was to provide her boss with an ultimatum—

give her an office and staff to pick up her work, or she would leave. Fortunately her company responded in kind, but all of this could have been addressed before the "promotion" took place.

Match your communication style to your organization.

One male HR executive I worked with for about seven years summarized his observations about working with female executives in his 20+-year career by saying that "women talk too much." He said it was particularly obvious to him when he was asked to speak at a panel on diversity in engineering and technology and he was the sole male on the panel. Not only have I heard this from other male executives, a woman executive I hired was drawn to speaking on the finest details, and she once told me that "as you can tell, I like to talk."

Talking and communicating are vastly different experiences in the workplace. The former leaves the listener with the option of tuning out because it's just talk. Even if you have valid, important concepts and facts to disseminate, not allowing quiet time for people to digest or ask questions will force them to tune out.

A great technique I picked up from one of my male direct reports is to start a conversation by saying, "I'm just talking here." He used this phrase to set expectations with the listener that he was thinking out loud, or brainstorming in an informal way so his opinions could be viewed as initial observations, rather than significant revelations based on a detailed analysis. This technique was very effective in preparing busy executives for a wandering conversation.

There are communication styles that women lean toward that are markedly different from men when it comes to getting to the point. Women have a tendency to "soft-sell" their ideas, particularly if their ideas and opinions veer from the norm. Women also like to be inclusive, and take time to highlight the contributions of others, again taking a longer route to making their ideas and conclusions known. There are probably many reasons for these behaviors, such as the need for women to put their peers at ease, or to point out how truly competent they are in a sea of biases. In a Club culture, women are obliged to continually reestablish their credentials and smarts while getting to the point. However, it's important for women to adjust their communication styles to be direct, make their points up front, and reference the basis for their opinions in order to be heard and to have an impact on decisions. As in my staying calm example, being too direct may not work if the environment doesn't foster open and honest discourse.

$-\square-$

In a Club culture, women are obliged to continually reestablish their credentials and smarts.

$-\square-$

Many coaching businesses have been spawned in the last 10 years to help women with communication skills within an executive peer group. My experiences with communication styles, as well as those of my colleagues, are that communication styles vary greatly. The three most significant things a woman — or any executive — can do is to *know when to listen*, then *actively listen*, and *solicit feedback* from others. Do you need a coach to improve your communication? I don't believe so. A mentor could be terrific in this regard, but in the absence of a mentor, careful thought will help adjust your style. Listening is the most important aspect of the communication process and one of the hardest things to master. It takes practice. Without it, we jump to conclusions and solutions without knowing the problem, and our biases and heuristics take over. Note, however, that adjusting your style is not the same as changing your style, which is often not possible considering your personality factors. Effective communication is not easy for either gender. It requires a willing listener and an environment that fosters and accepts open discourse and constructive feedback which focuses on the message rather than the person delivering it.

An interesting publication from 1983 called "Inside the Jury"[32] noted that a few people do the most talking during jury deliberation and therefore carry the most influence. Men were consistently found to speak more frequently than women during deliberations. This seems to be the adoptive norm in a group. Why, then, would the male HR executive described above believe that women talk too much? I suspect that being a minority male on a women's panel in a women's conference would shift the norm, and provide women with the comfort level to speak openly and often without having the burden of continually proving their value to the group.

To a larger degree, effective communication, at least in groups, requires strong group leadership to insure that all ideas are heard and discussed without impunity. The vast majority of board seats in for-profit companies are held by men. The biggest complaint against boards that oversaw the disastrous business scandals such as Enron, Tyco, and WorldCom was that the dissenting members did not speak up. For executive women in a Club-based culture, speaking up is an even greater challenge than refraining from speaking too much. Women have to be allowed to speak and allowed to be heard.

Develop rapport with a few individuals.

Remember, you're not in the Club, so don't attempt to get everyone to accept you. Target one or two individuals and find common ground. Take an interest in the interests of others, and yes, it may mean becoming familiar with sports lingo. At a minimum, be aware of what is important to your business and use that as a starting point for communications. What was the box office for the new releases over the weekend? What current events are impacting the economy and potentially the business? What unique interests do your peers or boss have? I've known people who competed in triathlons, raced cars and built houses. You can always find engaging topics to discuss with your peers if you understand their interests. You can't change your fundamental personality traits, nor can you increase your likability if you don't fit within the framework of the group, so expending a lot of effort trying to get the group to like you is wasted effort. However, everyone needs communication skills to lead people and companies. Company owners, subject matter experts, or Club members often advance without having those skills, and may surround themselves with people who have them. Ultimately those organizations risk long-term success. For women, communication skills are fundamental to advancing their careers.

Don't expect women to become your ally just because they are women.

I've hired and promoted hundreds of people in my career, and in a few cases terminated some as well. There will always be circumstances where a person on your team no longer matches the needs of the company or there is a shift in organizational goals, or even a shift in cultures. The average person holds some sense of loyalty or appreciation for the person who gave them their first title or their first opportunity in your organization. I have developed a long-lasting relationship with the majority of people I have hired or promoted, with a few exceptions of course.

– □ –

...recognize that men and women share similar human traits.

– □ –

In one IT organization with a strong Club culture, a woman I hired from a competitor quickly adapted to her position and did well as a newbie her first year. Her first appraisal was good, but her annual salary increase was very conservative (as she was one of the highest-paid executives in a group with one other female executive whose compensation was low compared to her male peers). She was also the newest person in the bonus pool and was competing against a Club favorite for limited bonus dollars. Over time, the female executive I hired began to undermine the team and disparage their work, including my work. Eventually her behavior drew the attention of the division head and HR, and she was called in to discuss her behavior.

It appeared she harbored such ill feelings about her raise and bonus, regardless of the context, that she felt personally harmed by the decision and attacked anyone associated with me or my team. She also felt harmed by the cost reduction efforts that were placed at her feet when she was hired. That circumstance was the luck of the draw and bad timing, but she didn't see it that way. (Without warning, the company had announced an aggressive IT cost reduction effort, and unfortunately that challenge came with the territory of being an IT executive.) The behavior of course reflected poorly on her, and closed the door to collaboration across teams. So, although I hired her, and eventually she moved into a higher-level position, she looked past the opportunities I did give her and instead continued to feel personally harmed. This was clearly an exceptional case, but it's important not to take your relationship with female peers or staff for granted, and recognize that men and women share similar human traits.

Insist on "synchronous collaboration."

By design, synchronous communication allows two systems to negotiate or "collaborate" on their particular settings before sending data to each other. The benefit of this type of communication is that it allows each system to set expectations with each other and facilitates a bi-directional flow of data. For women in executive positions, collaborating without synchronization can be detrimental to your success. Debra Lee, Chairman and CEO of BET Networks, broke out of the peer group ranks and became the boss in 1996, assuming a position where six of her eight direct reports were men. Ms. Lee was a key speaker at the Wall Street Journal's conference called "Women in the Economy" in early 2011. She believed that she was trying to be "nice" and inclusive when she took the reins of her CEO role by initially supporting her male executive team members. However, she realized that the men were not sharing information or involving her in the work of their divisions, which is typical of Club-based cultures, and eventually she had to replace them with a team that would support her.[33]

− □ −

...working alongside the Club, it's quite difficult to forge a collaborative equilibrium.

− □ −

To some degree, collaboration is a double standard. Women are expected to collaborate with everyone around them while their male peers are exempt from collaboration. I would consistently hear from my male executive peers in one of the Club-based organizations I worked in that my organization needed to be customer-focused and collaborative. What my staff quickly determined was that collaboration meant reacting to and performing work that was important to the Club, not necessarily to the strategies and goals of the company. The "collaboration" was also very one-sided, as Debra Lee discovered. When you're working alongside the Club, it's quite difficult to forge a collaborative equilibrium, but when you have the authority to change teams, you must do so.

Another woman executive I interviewed worked across a number of industries, as I have. As an IT executive working for a media and entertainment company in the mid-1990s, she observed that as long as any business unit was making its numbers, "anything was acceptable:" berating, complaining, undermining, and non-cooperating behaviors were all fair game. She, like countless other women executives, believed that professionalism and hard work would overcome the behavior. It didn't, and she moved onto another company. She also pointed out that the Club members who had a history of bad behavior would always be there, and her prediction has been accurate. That's where the collusion comes in, although no one really thinks of Club-based organizations as collusive. In a loose definition of the word, it can be, because Club behavior perpetuates exclusivity.

For example, I had hired a female IT executive to head the IT systems of a distribution business unit. From day one, the business unit executive team was not making it easy for her to win their confidence. There had been some miscommunication about a trip she took to Europe, where she briefly stopped in the London distribution office to discuss the potential for them to use a new system she was developing. After her trip, one of the business unit executives accused her of not being open and collaborative, because he wasn't aware of the nature of the meeting. According to her, he said he would "ream her a new one" if she ever did that again. She came into my office to resign after that conversation.

It wasn't the sole reason for the resignation, but it was the pivotal event that prompted her recognition that she was missing two key elements of success: synchronous collaboration, and adequate rapport with this individual. This unfortunate situation sounds dramatic and it felt that way at the time, so I was compelled to report it to the compliance officer, who in turn contacted the head of the business unit about the incident. The surprising part about this event was that it wasn't the first time this particular male executive had become aggressive. Yet, the Club culture allowed previous incidents, as well as this one, to pass and let him continue on in his position. Fortunately for the female IT executive, she recognized what she needed to be successful and made the right choice for her career. She returned to her previous company and gained a promotion!

Collaboration can only work if it is synchronous, and if you can't make that happen, you may have to move on to a more supportive environment.

CHAPTER 6:

Summary Points

☐ Do your best work every day regardless of the culture or political climate: Stick to your guns, work within your constraints and focus on diligence and quality.

☐ Match your work ethic to the business strategy and expectations of your role so you don't overwork and spend time in areas that are not important to you or your company.

☐ Take on new roles and assignments only when the work is supported up front

☐ Stay calm, carry on, and remain fierce: Block out the noise and stick to core management principles.

☐ Match your communication style to your organization: Be direct, make your points upfront, and reference the basis for your opinions.

☐ Develop rapport with a few individuals instead of trying to get everyone to like you.

☐ Don't expect women to become your ally just because they are women.

☐ Insist on synchronous collaboration.

CHAPTER 7 :

What Do Men Think?

ONE OF MY STATISTICS PROFESSORS IN GRADUATE school always found a way of challenging us while we poured through historical data. He taught us that one of the most important aspects of statistics is comparative analysis and the thought process that drives an analyst to look at data with one critical question in mind: "Compared to what?"

I, along with many of my female executive colleagues, have a distinctly female point of view of what our management experiences are like in corporate America and what it feels like to work in organizations that are predominantly managed by men. But how are our experiences viewed by our male counterparts, and what do men really think about working with, and for, women?

— □ —

*When women understand
what men think...they can make
better decisions.*

— □ —

When women understand what men think about women and what they expect from them in the workplace, they can make better decisions about their career choices and ambitions and have direct influence on shaping a successful career. I have compiled the male perspective from several sources: informal interviews and conversations, my work experiences over 30 years, the guidance provided to me by my mentors, and relevant news reports that reflect existing gender attitudes and behaviors. I met with a number of men at various levels in the corporate hierarchy across various-sized companies and found that their experiences and opinions about working with and for women were varied as well as thought-provoking, particularly with regard to the reasons they offered for excluding women from their Clubs. These perspectives represent the apex of the mountain, and offer an opportunity for others to delve deeper into their meanings and impact on business cultures and women's careers.

The positive side of the spectrum:

One young male director led the intellectual discipline of IT and Finance audit controls in a large corporation, and had a number of experiences working for women throughout his career. He didn't see women as a management class; rather he determined the efficacy of his boss based on his or her ability to provide clear vision and direction, and above all, the ability to be level-headed and logical. He happened to have very positive experiences with both male and female bosses.

One highly respected CFO was philosophical about woman executives. Gender just didn't matter to him. It was about the combination of credentials and experience that mattered the most in terms of a person's ability to lead and be successful. To him, graduating from a top-tier school (for example) said a lot about one's tenacity, intellect, and overall willingness to accept a challenge. He also offered the idea that if both men and women had a positive attitude, they would fare much better in their careers.

The idea of using positive thinking as a means for women to have more opportunities, or better opportunities, to lead organizations is intriguing to me. Is it possible that women exhibit less positive attitudes in the workplace and therefore are not only fighting gender biases but need to become more optimistic in their behaviors? According to Scott O. Lilienfeld and Hal Arkowitz, who wrote "Can Positive Thinking be Negative?,"[34] the cause and effect of positive thinking on careers and life experiences in general has yet to be proven. From my perspective, however, if someone is more optimistic and has a particular personality trait that makes them more likable or more confident in their decisions and leadership abilities, this may support the CFO's assertion. A common theme I hear from both men and women executives is that women need to become more confident about their abilities and interactions with men. Using a positive attitude as a spring-board toward confidence could certainly portray a woman as more competent and therefore more valuable to a firm.

A systems engineer who worked at one of the top technology manufacturing and consulting firms in the U.S. for over 25 years recalled having two female bosses in his career. Throughout his career, his company openly promoted diversity and fully supported gender parity, so the possibility of not accepting or supporting a woman because of her gender seemed remote in his frame of reference. He evaluated all of his bosses on the same criteria regardless of gender: his or her ability to manage situations and projects, and the ability to manage people. He believed that both of his female bosses had good management skills but one had better interpersonal skills, and he found his experience with her to be much more positive for him. He made it clear that his former male bosses weren't different from his female bosses as a class; they too were good at meeting one or both of the criteria that were most important to him.

Fortunately, there are senior executives who are strong advocates of gender diversity and actively seek women for their management teams and boards. I was very fortunate recently to meet a passionate *CEO and founder of a global technology services firm* who shared his unbiased attitudes toward women with me. This CEO leads over 35,000 employees in more than

40 countries, and he has over 20 years experience working alongside executive women.

He described his experiences with women as being the same as with men, and he even refuted the labor data indicating that women are not making much progress toward C-level positions and board positions. He appointed two C-level women to his senior management team and acknowledges this as the best reflection of putting his beliefs into practice. One of the two women runs worldwide sales, and the other is the company's CIO. He suggested that if women want to be in the C-suite, they have to get comfortable being around men and being themselves.

From his perspective, in the 21st century a clear delineation between work life, home life and social life no longer exists. In that construct, people react to each other as people, rather than as a man or woman in a particular corporate role, and there may be moments that could produce conflict or some other uncomfortable situation for either gender, just as you would expect in a family or social dynamic. Given that idea, this CEO contends that sexual harassment regulations have done more harm than good in terms of men wanting to have women around them in the workplace.

The CEO noted that it comes down to trust and being comfortable enough to have open and honest communication, while allowing men to be men. He doesn't believe in double standards for women, either. In a situational context, if a man loses his cool and gets aggressive in a meeting, a woman should be able to do the same without recourse. This CEO was quite remarkable in selecting his senior management team based on these principles, underscoring the need for more CEOs like him to create and foster a company culture that allows women to be women.

An IT enterprise architect at a large media conglomerate had worked for women across three different industries: banking, manufacturing, and media and entertainment. He didn't believe women had a unique management style that differentiated themselves from men; he felt that everyone has their own unique style. However, the distinguishing factor in his opinion between a good or bad leader was how competent they were in their ability to lead, articulate their vision, and charter, motivate, and develop their staff.

The few negative experiences he relayed were exclusively with male bosses and their overly aggressive, argumentative, and sometimes berating behavior that is still tolerated in some corporate cultures today. He also experienced the effect of the Club culture in a few of the companies he'd worked at, and he learned when to expend the effort to change the environment or win someone over versus when to accept that he "was never going to be in that Club."

In terms of industry experience, he clearly thought there was a visibly higher presence of women at senior levels of the organization while working for a leading toy manufacturer, compared to the scarcity of executive women in the media and entertainment company where he was currently working. He also believed there should be a more "balanced" representation of women in the workforce, considering they represent over half of the workforce. Lastly, he noted that he would like to see his daughters have the chance of following their ambitions without restraint from anyone.

I reconnected with a *board chairman and former CEO* whom I mentioned in an earlier chapter for an informal discussion about women executives. He completed two tours of duty with the armed forces and had an illustrious career spanning over 30 years in the banking and technology industries, which might suggest to some that he would hold a traditional view of women in the workplace. He felt that women are in fact working harder than men because they may have to overcompensate for the culture of their workplace, and because of the social context of women as less experienced leaders than their male counterparts. However, this Chairman remains keenly interested in supporting gender parity in the senior ranks, because of his desire to exploit talent regardless of gender. The issue also hits closer to home for him because of his advocacy for his daughter's academic and professional achievements. He believes she has the skills and talent to run a company some day, and he expects her to have an opportunity to do so.

An executive practice leader for one of the Big Four consulting firms worked for three women during his 20-year work history. He felt that by and large those experiences were different from working for men in the sense that they were more professional or "arm's length." He said the interactions with his male bosses were more personal and much more casual. They talked about sports or candidly coached one another. He suggested that his experiences could have been the result of his own style of interacting with women and not necessarily a reflection of how different women leaders are from men.

He also offered that the leadership styles of women that he'd observed tended to be more deliberate. The women executives looked like they were working hard at asserting themselves in their roles. He also described a sentiment I heard previously from another male executive: men face an increased risk working with and for women on "multi-dimensional facets." His point was that he can berate a man and, for example, say to him, "stop thinking from the right side of your brain, and stop acting like an idiot," and it wouldn't be an issue. In fact, the man would get it and continue to engage him. He said he couldn't say that to a woman without her having a "bad day," and without him facing "some consequence" for saying it. He said that he understood that there is an "unintended consequence" of making the work environment "safe" for women, but now women can wield significant power over men's careers and lives if they file charges of inappropriate behavior, whether it's legitimate or not. His advice to women is "excel at being a woman" and "don't be one of the guys." He believes there is unspoken respect regardless of cultural norms when women embrace the burden of higher standards and hold themselves up to those standards.

A *young senior financial analyst* for an energy trading company who recently completed his undergraduate studies and CPA certification had four years of work experience under his belt when we met to discuss his experience working with and for women. He had a unique view because he had had only two bosses in his career thus far; one woman and one man, and he clearly saw differences between the two. In his first job, he was the only male out of eight staff members on the accounting team his boss managed. He felt his female boss was very nurturing and really cared about developing the people around her. He also noted she was extremely smart and aggressive in a good way. She wouldn't shy away from issues and she "knew how to talk to people." He believes that men his age don't mind taking orders from women and believes it's part of the era they live and work in.

As for working with women, he echoed a previous sentiment from a male colleague of mine who was an HR executive —that some of the women were too "chatty" and too personal with him. He preferred to engage them on a professional level rather than a social level. In contrast, his current male boss was more "intense" and "to the point" and didn't convey much emotion or empathy for his workplace dilemmas; he knew that he would have to face those on his own. The other side of this, however, was that he was able to build a connection from his current male boss to the male traders in his company through their common interests in sports. There simply was a higher level of comfort and ease in networking with the traders than with his female co-workers, because he just had more in common with them.

Several of this young analyst's observations stood out during our interview with respect to tradeoffs that women make in their careers, double standards, and the organic ways Clubs are built. He noted that the front office positions at the trading desk were all men, while the back office positions were all held by women. He attributed that to women "settling" for lower-stress jobs, or jobs with less risk, while the men had more of a "killer instinct" and were willing to accept more risk. He had seen traders get very emotional on the trading floor, swearing and slamming phones when things didn't go their way, and he believed it would be acceptable for women to act the same way within the context of that environment. Whether the gender split between front office and back office was clearly due to women's interests or the biases we've seen associated with work roles that the culture finds acceptable for women, we won't really know if it would be acceptable for women to let loose on the trading floor until women achieve parity in those positions.

Generally though, the analyst found the traditional corporate back-office personnel to be more restrained in their behavior, and he expected both men and women to "hold back" their reactions and emotions. The observation that struck the common chord for me was in how his male and female bosses and peers evaluated new talent and ultimately formed the underpinnings of the company culture. "Woman bosses looked at skills, while men were looking if the person fit in" to the environment. For example, one woman his male boss interviewed for a finance position was highly qualified, but he found her to be very procedural and almost timid, which called into question her ability to be successful in an "intense" environment. The analyst also noted that the front-office staff was built from connections the traders made with each other at previous employers; they frequently shepherded their friends toward open positions in his firm. Once again, we see how easily men build connections among themselves, and the tremendous role mentorship plays in building their careers.

The not-so-nice end of the spectrum:

At the opposite end of the spectrum of attitudes was an **IT *vice president*** who had never worked for a woman. A reorganization resulted in him working for a woman who had previously been his peer, and he marched into HR and said, "I'm not about to start working for a woman now." Although a reorganization can wreak havoc with one's psyche, fundamentally I believe that this executive saw women as less competent than himself and likely felt his star quality was diminished by the experience. The company, on the other hand, missed an opportunity to recognize the flaws in their culture and raise the bar on behavioral expectations and benefits of working in a diverse organization.

Surprisingly, most of the men I interviewed were startled by this account and represented the opposite end of the spectrum. It could be that I tended to interview men that I thought were approachable and perhaps current in their thinking and behaviors toward women executives. I also pondered whether the interviewees inflated their attitudes of gender acceptance and inclusiveness and told me what I wanted to hear, but I ruled out the latter idea because the men with the strongest opinions and recommendations were very passionate, confident, and successful in their own right and weren't the least bit interested in a offering a politically correct opinion.

Although this next example is not specific to men working with or for women in the workplace, it reveals an ugly side of bias that can be nurtured through our educational system and ultimately carry over to the workplace. If young men hold certain views of women while in college, why wouldn't they take those views with them to the workplace?

Yale University was caught in a gender firestorm in early 2011 because one of their fraternities, the ultimate example of men's Club behavior, was reportedly chanting derogatory slogans on campus about women such as "No means yes" and "Yes means ass." For me, writing it is as vile as hearing it; it's clearly appalling on many levels. Dismissing the reported behavior as "frat boys being frat boys" calls into question the leadership at the institution.

In response to the article that brought attention to the Yale fraternity chant ("Men and Women at Yale, Is Boola Boola a Sexist Chant?"), the Letters to the Editor published in the Wall Street Journal (April 2011[35]) illuminate how opinions differ across gender lines based on the unique experiences women face in our culture. One gentleman from Arizona suggested that women should look to their peers in the Middle East and be appreciative for their job opportunities and education in America, and suggested they "enjoy and celebrate" the university rather than suing it. Another gentleman expressed relief that Yale couldn't be legally liable for a Title IX violation because they would have to prove the university administration deliberately acted with indifference to the women's complaints. In contrast, women who responded to the WSJ article called attention to how a woman perceives and feels aggression in the words and actions of men. They perceived the frat boy behaviors as threatening to their personal safety and their "ability to access education." A woman from Indianapolis highlighted a common theme I've heard from female executives, which is related to how the words and actions of male colleagues are received by women. She felt that the chants crossed the line from "brutish pleasure" for the men to "a lifetime of nightmares" for women.

The Wall Street Journal is under no obligation to provide a statistical sampling of the comments submitted to them by gender, and my intent in referencing the small sample here is to illustrate clear and current-day gender differences that echo the experiences of the women I interviewed. Men who are in The Club have no reference point or insight into women's experiences unless they've encountered similar threats and challenges.

A Different Perspective:

A few men whose wives were not in the workforce and were not pursuing professional careers offered their opinions about the gender disparity in leadership positions in the workplace.

One, a ***director of development*** for a top university, posed the question, "Are women even pursuing those positions?" He wondered whether women were actively vying for leadership positions, or if they were making other choices, such as his wife did, to remain at home with the children. His frame of reference was with his wife, and his wife's sisters who all acquired a degree, but chose not to pursue a career.

Another example, ***a medical doctor,*** said his wife held a high-level corporate job for over 10 years, and decided to take some time off. She returned to another high-level job after a few years, only to leave shortly afterward because she felt the expectations of the role and the workload were a burden, He speculated that she might have become "used to not working."

Although these scenarios relate to the choices women make throughout their lives—to have a career or not have a career—they may also reflect the "leaking" pipeline idea that women abandon their quest for executive leadership positions during their careers because of the external factors discussed throughout this book, such as Club cultures in corporate organizations, deep-seated biases, resistance, or the often noted child-rearing penalty that work against their chances to compete and succeed.

CHAPTER 8

Corporate and Societal Prescriptions for Women –
What Women Need Now

SO HOW DO WOMEN BREAK THROUGH The Club walls, get on the board or in the C-suite, and realize their leadership potential? Learn from others, leverage the critical elements of success, demand resources and support, be aware of your contributions and the external factors impacting your progress, and make informed choices that are right for you and your organization. Hopefully this book raised awareness of what worked for me throughout my career, and perhaps it will help expand the dialogue for the work ahead of all of us. Undoubtedly a number of external changes need to occur in our corporations and in our society to further capitalize on women's talents in the workforce.

Women must rekindle their activism to achieve a level playing field in the workplace. Men aren't off the hook for this activism either. An insightful observation by Dr. Mary Lou Schmidt was that men become interested in gender biases once it hits closer to home, such as when their daughters or wives are pursuing careers or experiencing Club biases. This was the case for my longtime mentor, who expects to see his daughter in a CEO position some day.

Many women, including myself, are hesitant to think of ourselves as activists, or even utter the word in public. It may feel strident to do so, considering how women have transitioned from the millions of factory and clerical jobs they held in the 1920s to the professions women inhabit in 2011. If you pause on those accomplishments though and look further at the historical data, less than 1% of women performing clerical work in the 1920s could be classified as managers, superintendents or officials.[36] Comparing that to 2010 labor data where 3% of CEO positions and 15% of Board positions are held by women, one sees that over the past 90 years, progress has been extremely slow in getting women to the top leadership positions, particularly given their academic achievements and professional experience.

I believe women haven't been present in the top positions or boardrooms in sufficient numbers because they've resolutely accepted the difficulties and hurdles of the female experience in the workplace as a common occurrence, and have accepted the burden of balancing work with personal responsibilities as if it were a biological principle that can't be tested or changed. Activism has to start with awareness and an educated work-force, by raising awareness in corporations, on Wall Street, and in academia. To some extent our federal regulators have to become more supportive of women's intellectual capital and contributions to the GDP by proactively gathering gender statistics that show the trends in leadership across all industries, including our government.

– □ –

...women...have accepted the burden of balancing work with personal responsibilities as if it were a biological principle.

– □ –

In order for women to be successful in leadership positions, corporations must embrace gender diversity throughout their organizations from the top down and the bottom up, and eliminate biases at the source. How can a board expect a woman to succeed as a senior manager or CEO in a company that doesn't have a proven track record in promoting women to senior-level positions? Rule one is you can't be successful if you're not accepted. Xerox and IBM are only a few examples of companies I've encountered that have made notable progress in preparing their organizations for a diverse leadership team.

Every company should be required to train its current management team on recognizing the biased Club behaviors outlined in this book. It won't stop the behavior from occurring, just as having four hours of government-mandated sexual harassment training every year doesn't prevent harassment, but the training will raise awareness of the subtle behaviors that block women from fully contributing their skills and talents in the workplace and ultimately destroy productivity and innovation. This does not imply that women should be held to different performance standards than men. Instead, I see awareness training as a way to educate an organization on how to remove the hurdles women experience in the workplace.

High schools should start promoting gender equality for their sports teams, and they should direct more of their female students to math, science, and engineering programs.

Undergraduate and graduate business programs need to infuse their curricula with research from departments within their own universities that are providing insights into gender biases, and the programs should address the biases. Many top universities conduct research in behavioral science, labor economics, and sociology as well as gender issues, but a wide gap remains between conducting and publishing the results in journals and books, and actually educating men and women in the workplace. Undergraduate and graduate business students are not exposed to relevant workplace research, nor are they prepared for resistant workplace behaviors and gender biases. Without that exposure, the next generation of leaders won't have the data to make the right choices within their companies.

In workplace environments, many executives are completely unaware of their own biases. Companies and boards are just starting to evaluate Club cultures and challenge the ways that executives and board members are selected, not because women are demanding it, but because shareholder oversight groups are questioning the practice after the decline of a large number of corporations during the financial crises. It's a hard code to break.

Entry onto boards still requires a man to lead the way and open the door. I'm surprised to see how many young women are appointed to boards because of the relationship their father has with the board. Unfortunately it still comes across as quid pro quo, rather than an appointment based on qualification. As I mentioned in Chapter 5, boards typically look for members with six or more years of board experience, which is rare for a woman to achieve since so few women have been on boards in recent years. But women have to start somewhere—even if it means coming into the board the same way their male counterparts have had for years, which is through a Club network.

There is an abysmal lack of mentors for women. Mentorship for women is a key success factor and needs to become more formalized in an organization's hierarchy. If you ask male executives if they've mentored women during their careers, most would say they have not done so, but there aren't yet enough women executives to mentor other women. We don't have the critical mass to do it alone. Although my own mentors became mentors because of our close working relationships and their desire to mentor others, I didn't find a mentor at every place I worked, particularly places with Club-based cultures. In hindsight, I've been the most successful when I had a mentor, and I had the best work experiences in more diverse environments.

Some women described to me what their work experiences were like without a mentor; they said it felt as if they were doing everything on their own, or like they were out on a tree limb while someone was chipping away at it. In other words, work is harder and career progress takes longer in the absence of a mentor. When I think of the young financial analyst's observation that men take more risks than women (Ch. 7), as well as the opportunities I had in my career, I feel that taking risks as a woman without a mentor can limit or even damage a woman's career if the results are not optimal.

Mentor programs need to start well before a woman enters the workplace. Women need mentors in high school and in particular, in our colleges and universities. Mentorship programs need to be formalized in our academic institutions in order to level the playing field with our male counterparts, who "organically" mentor each other. Southwest Air established a mentorship program in Boston targeted at grade school students called Adopt a Pilot.[37] The pilots teach the students on a wide variety of topics related to aviation and tie these topics to the students' core subject matters. Programs like this need to reach women so they can see themselves in leadership roles in any discipline.

In the absence of mentoring programs, women need to both seek out mentors and leverage their knowledge with each other. Women need to take on the responsibility of mentoring other women and offer their time to other women, informally or formally. I regularly schedule lunches and calls with women I mentor to check on their progress, offer advice, and brainstorm solutions to their concerns. I hope that this book and others like it will act as a guide in the absence of a mentor and will stimulate women to be proactive in starting mentorship programs in their own organizations.

As a start, all publicly traded companies should be required to publish the diversity statistics of their entire management team as well as their senior team and board members in their annual reports. Due to deep-rooted biases, most companies are unaware of their own statistics. A company policy that espouses antidiscrimination practices by itself is ineffective in combating gender biases. Publishing data and comparing companies' performance against that data is the only way to call attention to the grim realities of women's professional progress in the workplace.

There are women's organizations that publish lists of the best companies for women to work for and commend companies for their efforts in hiring and promoting women, but I'm advocating a stronger push to U.S. news consumers by calling for a comparative analysis such as that shown in the table in Chapter 5, for all of the Fortune 500 companies. Such an analysis would include the percentages of women on these companies' boards and on their senior management teams, to be released as part of the Fortune 500 rankings published each year.

The U.S. Department of Labor (DoL) should expand their reporting and include the diversity statistics from publicly traded companies, to monitor gender-based trends. There are companies that already compile this type of data and publish it for their client base (e.g., Catalyst, McKenzie), but this doesn't capture the media attention to the same degree as the DoL reports. Greater DoL involvement may also stimulate more economists to explore ways that the female labor pool can be better leveraged to increase job growth and meet marketplace demands. It's the broader audience that needs the awareness and needs to understand why they should care about the exclusion of women from leadership positions.

Gender biases must be rooted out during job placement. One male executive I interviewed suggested that organizations follow the hiring practices of large orchestras and conduct blind reviews of resumes by replacing names with a candidate number. If organizations are truly committed to rooting out gender bias, this practice should be applied to the hiring process periodically to monitor the degree of bias in the company. Companies can also benefit from overtly recruiting women for leadership positions. Overt recruiting may seem contradictory to the previous point, but the primary difference is that blind resume reviews can root out hidden biases, whereas overt recruiting sets an expectation for diversity within the company. There are many firms that specialize in diversity recruiting, and companies need to aggressively pursue these paths to rise above the hidden biases from their internal recruiters. Internal company recruiters and recruitment firms often collect diversity data during the online job application process, and they need to measure and report on how many women's resumes were actually reviewed and moved on to the next round of reviews. Given the studies and behaviors I discussed throughout this book, it seems likely that women's resumes are failing to garner the attention worthy of their accomplishments and are not rising to the hiring managers' attention. So, without significant changes to the hiring process, women will continue to be "rationally" eliminated from opportunities within companies.

Women need to bolster their confidence, keep their fear of failing in check, and take more risks. The woman executive I interviewed from a leading network service provider (Ch. 3) said that "women should never fear failure," and believed that "fear of failure is self-induced behavior." She offered "that women's mistakes seem to be more memorable only because there are fewer women in leadership positions." Economics tells us that there is an inherent relationship between risk and failure—the greater the risk, the greater the likelihood of failure. For women, this means having a strong commitment from their company and their boss to take on more risks in order to increase their scope of responsibilities.

CONCLUDING THOUGHTS

Where do we go from here? Women's contributions can't and shouldn't be shackled by outdated beliefs that their unique role as wives, mothers, and nurturers hinders them from achieving their professional aspirations or leading organizations. As I've contended throughout this book, the de-valuation of women's achievements, contributions, and experiences in the workplace stems from many behavioral and societal factors emanating from both genders. Women are on the precipice of retracting the slight gains they've made in ascending to leadership positions since they entered the workforce in droves 90 years ago. If women don't start raising their voices about the value of their education and work experiences, and raising awareness for gender disparity in the workplace and in society, we may face more intimidating consequences in the future.

— □ —

...we can make a difference...
It's time to raise your voices.

— □ —

Unless we dismantle The Clubs physically and psychologically, we won't see more women as film directors or producers, department chairs, management executives, CEOs, board directors, etc. While women can't change every aspect of human behavior and corporate organizational structures, we can make a difference for the generations to follow in terms of setting the tone and leading by example in all of our undertakings, and enlisting our male colleagues along the way. It's time to raise your voice, and your glass, to mentorship, activism, data-driven dialogue, unbiased hiring practices, more engaged Boards, better corporate awareness and governance, and forging a less arduous path to the top.

A C K N O W L E D G E M E N T S

I WANT TO THANK THE RESEARCHERS, professors, colleagues, and executives for sharing their experiences and opinions with me, as well as providing engaging conversation and thought-provoking ideas. I'd also like to thank my extraordinary mentors who lead by example—Frank Wapole and James Barlett—and the special friends, accomplished men and women, and family who also contributed their stories and opinions while encouraging me throughout the writing process. To my husband Paul, I offer the biggest thank you for being a great listener and supporter of my many passions.

Bibliography

Introduction – It's Not You

[1] In 1993, women represented 7.53% of 7,422 board directors from Fortune 1000 boards. Journal of Management Dec. 2002. 28:747, Women and Racial Minorities in the Boardroom.

In 2010, women CEOs were present in 3% of Fortune 500 companies, as published by money.ccn.com magazine.

[2] Based on 2011 census figures. www.census.gov/compendia/statab/cats/education.html

Chapter 1: The Club – In Corporate Organizations and Everywhere Else

[3] Colvin, Geoff. (2008) *Talent Is Overrated: What Really Separate World-Class Performers from Everybody Else*. New York, NY: Penguin Group.

[4] Technolink Association, a coalition of aerospace, academic, defense, energy, life sciences, innovation, public safety, and international and policy leaders bridging the public and private sectors to develop a virtual high technology corridor in Southern California.

[5] Dr. David Lewin, Neil H. Jacoby Professor of Management, Human Resources & Organizational Behavior, UCLA Anderson School of Management, May 2011 lecture "Compensation Committees: Strategy, Pay-for-Performance, Recommendations."

[6] "BLS Spotlight on Statistics Women At Work," http://www.bls.gov/spotlight/2011/women/; March 2011, U.S. Bureau of Labor Statistics.

[7] Goldin, Claudia, and Cecilia Rouse. 2000. "Orchestrating Impartiality: The Impact of "Blind" Auditions on Female Musicians." American Economic Review, 90(4): 715–741.

[8] Toder, N. L. (1980), The Effect of the Sexual Composition of a Group on Discrimination Against Women and Sex-Role Attitudes. Psychology of Women Quarterly, 5: 306-307. doi: 10.1111/j.1471-6402.1980.tb00963.

[9] Cornwell, Erin York and Hans, Valerie P. "Contextualizing Jury Participation: Case, Jury, and Juror-Level Predictors of Participation in Jury Deliberations," Cornell University (abstract).

Chapter 3: Club Behaviors – Lethal Barriers to Entry and What to Do to Meet the Challenge

[10] Sunstein, Cass R. and Hastie, Reid. Four Failures of Deliberating Groups. John M. Olin Law & Economics Working Paper No. 401 (2nd Series) April 2008; http://www.law.uchicago.edu/Lawecon/index.html

[11] Schilt, K. (2010) *Just One of the Guys? Transgender Men and the Persistence of Gender Inequality*. Chicago: University of Chicago Press.

[12] Heidrick & Struggles International, a worldwide executive search firm, specializing in chief executive, board of directors, and senior-level management assignments.

[13] Kelly, Maura. "A Quota for Female Executives," PARADE magazine, July 13, 2010. http://www.parade.com/news/intelligence-report/archive/100613-a-quota-for-female-executives.html

[14] Steinpreis, Rhea E., "The Impact of Gender on the Review of the Curricula Vitae of Job Applicants and Tenure Candidates: A National Empirical Study" (1999). ADVANCE Library Collection. Paper 269.

http://digitalcommons.usu.edu/advance/269

[15] Schilt, K. (2010) *Just One of the Guys? Transgender Men and the Persistence of Gender Inequality*. Chicago: University of Chicago Press.

[16] Gee, M.V. and Norton, S.M.. Thought & Action, The NEA Higher Education Journal. Fall 2009, 163–170.

[17] Morrissey CS, Schmidt ML. Fixing the system, not the women: an innovative approach to faculty advancement. J Womens Health (Larchmt). 2008 Oct;17(8):1399-408.

[18] Per Walmart's web site, May 2011: http://walmartstores.com/Diversity/302.aspx

[19] Wal-Mart Stores, Inc. v. Dukes et al. June 2011. http://www.supremecourt.gov/opinions/10pdf/10-277.pdf Stephen Bryer was the only male Justice to join in the dissent. Chief Justice John Roberts and Justices Anthony Kennedy, Clarence Thomas and Samuel Alito agreed with Justice Scalia.

[20] Wall Street Journal, "Justices Curb Class Actions," Jess Bravin, Ann Zimmerman, June 21, 2011; LA Times, "Wal-Mart bias case blocked by high court," David Savage, Salvador Rodriguez, June 21, 2011.

[21] Volume I, Three Mile Island, A report to the commissioners and to the public; Mitchell Rogovic, Director, George T. Frampton Jr., Deputy Director, NRC Special Inquiry Group, 1980.

[22] Kanter, R.M. (1993) *Men and Women of the Corporation*. New York: BasicBooks.

Chapter 4: It Starts at the Top – Acceptance of Club Culture in an Organization

[23] Lecture by Professor David Lewin, UCLA Anderson School of Management, May 2011, "Compensation Committees: Strategy, Pay-for-Performance, Recommendations."

Chapter 5: Getting to the Core of Club Behavior – How to Spot It Before You're Hired

[24] "Targeting Inequity: The Gender Gap in U.S. Corporate Leadership," Testimony to U.S. Joint Economic Committee, Ilene H. Lang, Catalyst, Sept. 28, 2010. http://jec.senate.gov/public//index.cfm?a=Files.Serve&File_id=90 f0aade-d9f5-43e7-8501-46bbd1c69bb8

[25] Ibid.

[26] Fortune 500, 2011 annual ranking of America's largest corporations, as listed on www.money.cnn.com. Executive management and board of directors data derived from annual reports published by the companies. Companies with more than five top executives are parenthetically noted.

[27] "Targeting Inequity: The Gender Gap in U.S. Corporate Leadership," Testimony to U.S. Joint Economic Committee, Ilene H. Lang, Catalyst, Sept. 28, 2010. http://jec.senate.gov/public//index.cfm?a=Files.Serve&File_id=90 f0aade-d9f5-43e7-8501-46bbd1c69bb8

[28] Based on a skills comparison conducted by xCeo Inc. for the author, 2011.

[29] Bloomberg Business Week, January, 2011 http://investing.businessweek.com/research/stocks/private/snapshot.asp?privcapId=3 5867

[30] The Meyers-Briggs Type Indicator (MBTI) was developed by Katharine Cook Briggs and Isabel Briggs Meyer in 1944 to assess personality traits with regard to attitudes and preference. The MBTI is often used in professional development, leadership training, and career counseling. https://www.cpp.com/products/index.aspx

Chapter 6: Tips from the Front Lines – Critical Elements of Success

[31] From "For Great Leadership, Clear Your Head," by Joshua Ehrlich, HBR Blog network, September 14, 2011. http://blogs.hbr.org/cs/2011/09/for_great_leadership_clear_you.html

[32] Hastie R, Penrod SD, Pennington N. (1983) *Inside the Jury*. Cambridge, Harvard University Press, pp. 141-142.

[33] Wall Street Journal, 4/11/11, "A Blueprint for Change," Women in the Economy. An executive task force. Rebecca Blumenstein.

Chapter 7: What Do Men Think?

[34] American Scientific Mind magazine, June 7, 2011.

[35] http://online.wsj.com/article/ SB10001424052748703789104576273790492118886.html

Chapter 8: Corporate and Societal Prescriptions for Women – What Women Need Now

[36] Kanter, R.M. (1993) *Men and Women of the Corporation*. New York: BasicBooks. Ch.1, The Evolution of Office Work for Women.

[37] Spirit Southwest Airlines magazine, October 2011, p. 165.

— □ —

*This book is dedicated to
my mother Olga,
who taught me the meaning of
strength and determination.*

— □ —

EAST BATON ROUGE PARISH LIBRARY

3 1 6   5 9 0 3   8 7 1 3 8 8 5

DISCARD

East Baton Rouge Parish Library
RIVER CENTER BRANCH

JUL 0 1 2013